THE
BELGIAN
HAMMER

Forging Young Americans
into Professional Cyclists

DANIEL LEE

FOREWORD BY
GEORGE HINCAPIE

BREAKAWAY BOOKS
HALCOTTSVILLE, NEW YORK
2011

The Belgian Hammer: Forging Young Americans into Professional Cyclists
Copyright 2011 by Daniel Lee

ISBN: 978-1-891369-91-9
Library of Congress Control Number: 2011927400

Published by Breakaway Books
P.O. Box 24
Halcottsville, NY 12438
www.breakawaybooks.com

FIRST EDITION

Contents

Foreword

I still remember my first trip to Europe. I was fourteen or fifteen years old and going over to France to do some races with the US national team. I had been riding my bike since I was eight, but this was going to be the first time I would get to race in some real competition.

What I found out right away was that the races were hard. The competition was more substantial than any racing we did in the United States. Guys like Daniele Nardello and Marco Serpellini were really strong and already had good tactical sense. But surprisingly, I found out that I was definitely on par with the Euros and did pretty well. That first trip gave me encouragement to believe I could succeed in cycling as a career.

In cycling, success at a young age often comes from within. But certainly, outside influences played a big role for me. My dad, Ricardo, and brother, Rich, have been my biggest mentors. My dad really helped me get to the next level. We would ride together every weekend and he would take me to the races. Even today, he still rides with me when he can. He loved cycling. It was his life. I saw how much he loved it and I just gradually grew into the same mind-set. It was a family sport for us. It may be hard to believe now, but when I first started out, I was kind of a lazy little kid. But I saw how much fun it was to win races and be part of the competition. Once I got hooked, I never looked back.

The next generation of American cyclists racing in Europe today has it much different than it was for me nearly twenty years ago. Guys like Taylor Phinney, Andrew Talansky, Peter Stetina, and Ben King are putting so much excitement on the horizon. And it's my goal to personally make sure that the pipeline of talent from the United States to Europe continues. The Hincapie Sportswear Development Team that my brother and I started is a way to help bring along young cyclists in Greenville, South Carolina, and see if they can make it to the next level. It's been very satisfying to help mentor Craig Lewis from an early age. Now he's racing professionally. Chris Butler graduated from the Hincapie Sportswear team to join me on the BMC Racing Team in 2010. Those are two success stories I am proud to have been a part of and both have a bright future.

The nice thing for any American racing in Europe today is that people in the United States are starting to realize there are other races besides the Tour de France. Obviously, the Tour is the biggest and best-known race. But thanks to the Internet and the growing mainstream popularity of the sport, the classics and shorter stage races are getting some good attention, too. While those guys might not get the worldwide media attention like you do from winning the Tour, they can have a long, high-profile career by being successful in other races.

If I had the opportunity to share a message with each and every young cyclist who dreams of being a pro racing in Europe, it would be this: Keep working hard. Keep believing. Always try to listen to your body and don't overdo it. It's easy to burn out at an early age if you don't pace yourself. And try to always train with someone who has been around for a while—someone who can mentor you along.

Keep riding,
George Hincapie

Photo courtesy of Hincapie Sportswear

Dedicated to:
Jennifer, my loving wife and eternal college sweetheart . . .
and Paul, Anna, and Bethany, our children, our inspiration.

Inspired by:
The simple notion that the future is always with the young.

Prologue: Easter in Bruges

My train rolled to a stop in the predawn darkness of Easter Sunday at the northern Belgian city of Bruges—starting point later that morning for the Tour of Flanders. The race, known locally in Dutch as the Ronde van Vlaanderen, is the biggest of the year in this small slice of Northern Europe where cycling matters most. Huge frigid raindrops pelted me as I stepped through the small open-air gap between the train and the covered station platform. The straps from my overstuffed duffel bag and laptop briefcase dug into my shoulders as I trudged into the station's main corridor.

I had come to Belgium from my home in Indiana in search of the soul of cycling: one writer's quest to discover what it takes for young Americans to make it in European professional cycling; what it takes to chase Tour de France dreams. The answers were all around me on the bumpy and narrow roads of Flanders and Wallonia—Belgium's Dutch- and French-speaking regions—as I watched races and interviewed some of my nation's brightest cycling prospects.

But for the moment, I was simply cold and tired. The previous day I had been soaked to my core while watching Taylor Phinney power away in the final two kilometers from an elite field of racers aged under twenty-three to win a stage of the Triptyque des Monts et Châteaux in Wallonia. Tom Boonen won at Monts et Châteaux on his path to cycling stardom. So did pros Stijn Devolder and Karsten Kroon. Few American cycling fans have heard of this race. But winning here can get riders on the path to a Tour de France–bound team.

Phinney crossed the finish line, his long arms spread wide, his mouth transforming from a smile to a scream as he rolled by just a few feet from where I stood. A few seconds later, the pack sprinted home in a twisted hypothermic frenzy. If someone had showed me a photo of just those riders' faces—the whites of their eyes piercing through grimaces blackened with mud and grime—I would have guessed they were trauma victims in shock. Perhaps they were: The racers had just spent four hours in driving rain, temperatures in the forties and wind gusts that easily topped twenty-five miles an hour. A couple of Belgians abandoned their bikes just after the finish line and ran into their nearby team bus for warmth.

Phinney, the American, was the victor on a miserable Belgian day.

That night in Izegem, the Belgian town that is the base for USA Cycling's National Development Team, I slept fully clothed in an attempt to regain warmth in a bed covered by a single comforter. The next day I arrived, still exhausted, at the small train station in Izegem at 6 AM for the forty-or-so-minute train ride to Bruges.

After my journey, I stopped at a café in the Bruges station for a chocolate pastry and coffee before stepping back into the cold rain.

"How do I get to the market square for the start of the bike race?" I asked a pretty blonde behind the counter.

"Down the walking path to the big brick building and turn right onto the shopping street," she said quietly with a shy smile and nod. She was attractive without wearing much makeup; friendly but reserved. That Flemish simplicity stood in contrast with the flamboyancy of what I had always considered to be Europe's other traditional cycling epicenter, Italy.

My mood began to improve even as my soaked jeans clung to my calves while I walked. Taylor Phinney had thrived in miserable weather the day before. I found the press room in the Hallen Markt, or market hall, under the famous and towering Belfry of Bruges. Just in front of this grand old building was the giant stage where each racer would have to pass through for the official sign-in for that day's Tour of Flanders. The most famous racers—Lance Armstrong and Tom Boonen among them—were stopped by the host for interviews. Over the next couple of hours, accordion-and-drum-driven Belgian beer-drinking music filled the air between the interviews to entertain the thousands of fans who crowded into

Bruges's medieval square.

"Who do you think will win?" I asked the woman behind the press table. I expected her to say *Tom Boonen*. After all, he was Belgium's face of cycling — an "A" list celeb who is part sports hero, part gossip heartthrob in this nation of 10.5 million, especially in Flanders, which makes up more than half of that population. "I like Hincapie," she responded, referring to the popular veteran American racer George Hincapie. The 360-plus media credentials granted this year were more than in the past couple of years because of the presence of Lance Armstrong, she added as she dug out a press packet from the mass of credentials.

I looped my official (and, thankfully, rain-resistant) Ronde van Vlaanderen media credential around my neck and set out to explore the press room. My thoughts drifted to how Americans had changed professional cycling since I'd started following the sport in the mid-1980s. Greg LeMond and Armstrong brought new bikes, aerobars, bravado, big money, and global attention to the sport. Americans, especially Floyd Landis, also contributed to the sport's seemingly endless doping scandals.

I nudged past burly motorcycle drivers dressed in boots and rain gear for what looked to be a treacherous day ferrying about photographers and cameramen on twisting or cobbled roads. Finally, at the back of the room, I had reached the press buffet: two- or three-foot piles of rolls, meats, cheeses, and pastries. Knowing that pro bike races last six-plus hours, I grabbed an orange juice, bread and cheese, and my second chocolate pastry of the young day.

It was just after this carbo-loading that I saw Phil Liggett, the raindrops still shimmering on his rain jacket. He held two coffees, one for him and one for his longtime cycling broadcast partner, Paul Sherwen. Having heard his smooth British voice for decades on TV cycling broadcasts, I approached Liggett like an old friend and told him my story: I was a reporter from Indiana who had raced briefly as an amateur in Belgium years ago. I was working on a book about what it takes for young Americans to make it in European professional bike racing.

He listened intently and replied, "And you came all this way?"

Yes, Flanders was the place I needed to be to tell the story of a new generation of Americans in European cycling. I talked about Taylor Phinney's daring win in the rain the day before. Liggett's face lit up, and he called out to the approaching Sherwen about Phinney's victory. Decades earlier, I had listened to Phil announce as Taylor's father, Davis Phinney, sprinted to two stage victories in the Tour de France.

Not wanting to be a pest, I quickly asked someone nearby to snap a photo of me with Liggett and headed back into the market square.

Clouds hung over the spires and steep-pitched roofs of the colorful buildings of Bruges. But the rain had stopped. TV helicopters—the universal signal that a big-time bike race is near—whirled above.

Just five Americans were among the 198 starters in this Tour of Flanders: Armstrong and Hincapie, the aging veterans; Tyler Farrar, the rising star; Steven Cozza, a young rider groomed on the international amateur circuit; and Jackson Stewart, who rose from the US racing circuit to also compete in the famed Paris–Roubaix.

Top-level cycling is still very European, a sport played out in a culture as foreign to Americans as a Friday-night high school football game would be to a Belgian kid.

It was only a little more than a generation ago, in 1981, that Jonathan Boyer became the first American to compete in the Tour de France. Since then, American riders have won an impressive ten Tours. But just two men, LeMond with three and Armstrong with seven, are responsible for that total. Consider that, as of 2010, only thirty-six Americans have competed in the Tour de France since the world's greatest bicycle race began in 1903, according to the Tour's historical database. That's only three times more than the twelve Americans who have walked on the moon.

Indeed, for an American cyclist to break into European professional cycling and reach the Tour de France is to venture into a strange new world. The Americans who rise to the top of the sport form a small circle, athletes who have overcome brutal odds. Those looking to forge careers as pro racers face a long apprenticeship in Europe and in America's ragged domestic racing scene.

Bruges before the start of the Tour of Flanders. Photo by Daniel Lee

Belgians enjoy the Tour of Flanders. Photo by Daniel Lee

Belgium, with its rain-filled days and aggressive amateur racing, is the perfect proving ground for this very international sport.

The scene has played out many times over the past quarter century: A young jet-lagged American arrives in the Brussels airport. He drags a bulky bike box and suitcase to the train platform and counts on strangers to watch his bike, or help him navigate the Belgian rail system as he finds his rented room. The tired American gazes out the train window at this new land, first at the graffiti-scarred railway corridors of Brussels and then villages populated by plain brick houses with tile roofs and horses roaming small pastures.

Yet American cyclists also feel connected here. People understand their sport. Newspapers carry photos of bike racers, not NFL players. A racer here doesn't have to explain to people what drafting is, or deal with angry drivers spraying them with Mountain Dew on some back road.

It was now about ten o'clock on Easter morning, and the Ronde van Vlaanderen began. The riders, bundled in arm and leg warmers for the chilled damp air, rolled out of Bruges's majestic market square for their one-day 162-mile journey over fifteen cobbled climbs. The motorcycles and team cars of the race caravan roared to life. Just then a bell tolled to celebrate the race's start, or to call parishioners to Easter Mass. I didn't know which. The bell's tone was deep, methodical, and meaningful.

Bong, bong, bong.

The rain that a few hours before had soaked and depressed me at the train station was gone. The skies had cleared. I stood shoulder-to-shoulder with the great throng gathered for Belgium's greatest bicycle race.

Bong, bong, bong.

The Tour of Flanders's 198 riders, the chosen few Americans among them, disappeared from sight. Their road ahead was narrow, dangerous, and demanding. I turned and walked over the wet cobblestones toward my Belgian host's car to follow their journey.

Davy Crockett Goes to Flanders

Davy, Davy Crockett, king of the wild frontier!
—"The Ballad of Davy Crockett"

As a boy, I listened to that song many times on a vinyl record I had of Disney's *Davy Crockett* show starring Fess Parker as the famous American pioneer. But on July 5, 1992—when I was a cycling-obsessed twenty-three-year-old—it simply struck me as odd to hear that tune crackling from the PA system minutes before my first Belgian bike race.

I rolled up to the start line in Merelbeke, in the East Flanders section of Belgium—the heartland of European cycling. A man sold sausages from a cart near the racecourse as I took my place amid the sixty-five other racers. I looked around to see rivals with unfriendly glares and oiled-up tree-trunk legs. Some were gnarled veterans, others baby-faced Belgians in their late teens or early twenties.

Davy Crockett quickly disappeared from my mind as the race began: My existence narrowed to the wheel in front of me as we sprinted down a Flemish street, over a thin strip of cobblestones. An approaching turn took us from a wider road to a narrow lane—a twelve-foot-wide artery clogged with dozens of cyclists. Brakes jammed. Midway back, I watched the leaders sprint out of a corner I was still slowing down to enter. My heart pounded, not from excitement but from oxygen debt. A mixture of sweat, spit, and snot began to cover my face.

Years later I would think back to the Davy Crockett song. I realized it was a perfect soundtrack: Europe, especially Belgium, has long been cycling's rugged frontier. For more than a generation, young American riders—driven by dreams and in search of adventure—

have been reverse pioneers of sorts. Americans venture to the Old Country to experience organized-but-torturous amateur racing. For a select few, it's a crucial step to making a living aboard their bikes. For most, it's a realization they aren't one of the select few.

My Athletes in Action cycling team arrived in Ghent, in East Flanders, on July 3, 1992. The team was exhausted from a thirty-six-hour journey that started in Ohio, passed through Germany, and included an unintended detour into the Netherlands. We found a small Greek restaurant and devoured cheese pizzas and pita bread as fast as the one woman in the place could prepare them. A couple of teammates, outgoing friendly guys, jumped behind the counter to help. As midnight passed, the more than a dozen riders on our team were spread over eight floors in a dormitory at a university in Ghent. We were joined by students from around the globe: Africa, India, China, across Europe. In room 220, I climbed into bed, my half-assembled bike beside me.

"The team is a little grumpy, tired, and disorganized now. That should change when we start racing," I wrote in my journal that night. "I'm nervous about racing—the cobbles. I want to do well so bad."

My journey to race in Europe had started six years earlier. In 1986, I didn't date, was cut from my high school baseball team, and brought home report cards filled with C's and D's. Then, along with high-school buddies Jim and Brooks, I discovered that something I had always loved to do—ride my bike—was actually a competitive sport. Network TV showed the Tour de France, or at least synthesizer-music-filled weekend highlights of it, as a spunky California kid named Greg LeMond overcame French teammate Bernard Hinault to become the first American winner. Another American, Andy Hampsten, was fourth. Davis Phinney, a studly sprint star with guns for biceps, was part of the ragged but inspiring 7-Eleven squad, the first American-based team to compete in the Tour.

My parents bought me my first racing bike—a Schwinn Tempo—

in 1987, the year I purchased my first racing license from the US Cycling Federation. I shaved my legs and felt like a man. At Ball State University in Muncie, Indiana, I trained 150, 200, and then up to 300 miles a week.

Being a bike racer meant having a good reason to abstain from my fraternity brothers' whiskey-and-fried-food-filled world of debauchery. I ate Fig Newtons and wheat spaghetti. I screamed down a Georgia mountain at fifty-seven miles an hour in the 1992 national collegiate championships. I crashed twice in one race on rain-slicked roads near *The Indianapolis Star*, the newspaper where years later I'd earn a living as a journalist. The first fall, on my right side, was a chain-reaction crash that left me curled against another racer on the pavement almost like we were spooning together in bed. Then, after knocking my seat back into place and rejoining the pack, I hit a slick painted line on the road and slid across the street on my left side, my Ironman watch and patches of skin ripped from my body with one motion.

But races weren't enough to satisfy my bike-riding addiction: I volunteered for cycling-related studies at Ball State's human performance lab—a chance to earn cash and learn about my body. I rode a stationary bike for two hours in a high-humidity chamber, a thermometer probe in my rectum to monitor my core body temperature and needles jabbed periodically into my arm to check blood sugar or other measurements. Another time, I endured a bendable plastic tube inserted in my nose, down my throat, and into my stomach for a "gastric-emptying" study—I gulped sports drink and pedaled. After a set time, the researcher sucked out the remaining fluids from my stomach to see how much of the liquid had been emptied from my gut.

I was a strong (at least when hydrated) though not remarkably gifted rider. My body fat registered less than 10 percent. My VO_2 max, or my maximum oxygen uptake, measured at 59, 64, and 69 ml/kg/min in three different tests, according my memory and training notes. That's enough to compete in tough races, especially considering that the average sedentary male had a VO_2 max of just 42. But it was far below top champions such as five-time Tour de France winner Bernard Hinault, at 88, and American Greg LeMond, at 92 to 94.

By the time I headed to Belgium, I was a lean six-foot-one, 158 pounds, and in the best shape of my life. As I drifted to sleep that first night in Belgium I listened, on cassette tape, to U2's *Achtung Baby* and thought about how I was living a dream.

The next day, July 4, our team departed the Ghent dorm for our first ride in Belgium, soon reaching narrow cobblestone streets. Each stone was roughly the size and shape of a small loaf of petrified bread, with jagged edges. The gaps between the stones were what made them so rough and tricky to ride. My front tire skipped over the stones, seemingly sliding into every possible gap between the ancient rocks. Rain fell.

We pedaled fifteen kilometers, or about nine miles, from Ghent's medieval-looking city center to watch a "kermis" race in a nearby town. This raucous form of racing is the soul of Belgium cycling. The word *kermis,* sometimes spelled *kermesse,* means "fair." Each summer, towns across the Flanders section of Belgium put on races as part of festivals or just to have an entertaining sports event. These multi-lap events twist through villages and countryside on small circuits, typically seven or eight kilometers per lap, with races sometimes lasting more than a hundred kilometers. The circuits often include a stretch of cobblestones and passages over single-lane farm roads. Kermises are like hockey fights: herky-jerky affairs where skill, strength, and intimidation commingle.

Clad in red, white, and blue jerseys, we drew stares from some of the hundreds of fans who lined the race circuit for this Saturday-afternoon kermis. We hoped seeing a Belgian race would somehow prepare us for our own race the next day.

The pack approached: A lead official car, then forty-four tightly grouped riders jockeying for position, then an ambulance (standard protocol for Belgian races). The road was roughly twelve feet wide in most places. A few of us jumped on the back of the caravan for one of the two-and-a-half-mile laps to get a sense of the speed of the race. We averaged about twenty-eight miles per hour for that snippet of what was a seventy-mile race. Fast.

In the United States, amateur racing is governed by USA Cycling. Riders compete in a strict system of five categories assigned according to experience and ability. Category 5s are beginners; Category 1s are the most accomplished racers. In Belgium, everyone competes in a single category: *liefhebbers,* or amateurs. I'd always likened this system to the famed single-class high school basketball tournament in my adopted home state of Indiana, where small schools and big schools for decades competed for one title. Like the old Indiana high school tournament, made famous in the movie *Hoosiers,* Belgian racing derives much of its beauty from its simplicity and connection to the culture.

Belgium also is unusual among Western European nations in that it welcomes individuals, not just teams, from foreign nations to join its kermises. It's a welcome mat to brutality. Kermis standouts, wherever they're from, can land pro contracts because of the intensity and reputation of these races.

Start lists for kermises I rode in Belgium contained plenty of local names: Joris Van Kerkhove of Ghent and Jaak Eechhout of Melle. Joining them were riders from the United States, Scotland, Ireland, New Zealand, Great Britain, the Netherlands, South Africa, and Australia.

In America, being a bike racer meant trying to find races within a reasonable drive—typically no more than about five hours for me—and then looking for buddies to share the cost of gas money. We'd carbo-load at Fazoli's. In Belgium, a rider could race just about every day through the summer within easy cycling distance. Race registration could be in a school, bar, or sports hall. Entry fees were cheap, the equivalent of about $3 when I was there, and some of that was for the deposit for your reusable race number. Unlike in the States,

Author nervous but smiling before kermis race in 1992.
Photo courtesy of Daniel Lee

riders in Belgium had to bring their own safety pins to attach their numbers. Fans lined every course. Fathers watched sons. Old pot-bellied men in wool cycling kits rode old steel bikes with exposed brake cables. Fans ran out of taverns to watch the riders pass, then headed back in to await the next lap.

My first race was the "Merelbeke–Kwenenbos" kermis. It was *16 ronden van 7.3 kilometers*: sixteen laps of a roughly four-and-a-half-mile circuit, including a strip of cobbles, for a total of about seventy-two miles. The race started under gray skies.

In bike racing, the more bunched together the riders are across the road, the easier the pace. Single file means the race is all-out, or in cycling lingo: The hammer is down. Belgians were always in single file, it seemed. If a chase group of twenty guys is trying to bridge up to a breakaway, they won't bridge up together but with twenty separate lung-burning attacks. Even if the pack was in a bunch, the speed still seemed high. In order to perform well, a rider must conserve energy by staying in the protective draft of the pack. But the spastic nature of the Belgians, especially in the race's opening miles, made that difficult.

Early in one kermis on a flat course, I glanced down at my computer: forty miles an hour, a speed typically reserved for descents or sprint finishes.

I wrote in my journal that it must be a hobby of the Belgians to intimidate Americans. Racers would hurl Dutch words at us we had no chance of understanding, yet we knew they were curses. Americans who suffered flat tires on cobblestones were laughed at by fellow racers and even fans.

We suffered humiliations yet tried to be aggressive. In my second kermis, I rode near the front. A big redheaded Australian launched a solo attack. I launched my own sprint from the pack to bridge up to him. Other riders followed. Sensing that his attack was being nullified, the Australian popped his brakes—perhaps angry because I sat just inches from his rear wheel. His abrupt drop in speed set off a chain reaction.

My front wheel hit the redheaded Australian's rear wheel. My head slammed into his back. I drove my helmet-covered forehead into the middle of his back in an attempt to gain the leverage to stay upright. Crashes happen in an instant. But racers also experience a horrible slow-motion realization that they're going down.

Somehow I emerged upright. It would have been a nasty crash: an initial impact followed by half a dozen or so riders plowing into me.

"F---ing a--hole!" I screamed, glaring at the Australian.

In America, the redheaded Australian would be an outcast for such a stunt. In Belgium, I didn't know the unwritten rule: Fend for yourself. I was the villain. Riders passed me yelling curses, pushing me, and making angry hand gestures.

After the race, several of my teammates struck up a conversation with the Australian. From what I remember, it was mostly talk about the race and the purpose of our team. We were a team of Christian athletes on a mission trip. I took that seriously, still do. But I couldn't bring myself to talk with him.

Court Maple, my roommate and cycling buddy from Ball State,

spent that summer racing elsewhere in Belgium. In a June 1992 letter, he wrote: "The Belgians don't speak a whole lot of English, practically none. There's nothing like racing when you don't know what the hell is going on! What the time gap is? When the primes [lap prizes] are? How many circuits to do at the end . . . Just have to go w/ the flow. Normally means nervousness + bizerk!"

I read his words from my fraternity house back in Indiana a few weeks before I headed to Belgium. Court, based in the town of Halle, later would tell tales of encounters similar to my run-in with the redheaded Australian. One involved a muscle-bound Belgian—Jean-Claude Van Damme on a bike, only taller—edging him off the road . . . elbowing, pushing, flicking him into the gutter. He screamed Dutch curse words, then demonstrated his fluency with the English F-word. He wanted the same wheel Court drafted behind. He wouldn't get it. Court jutted out his right elbow and knee in response. The big Belgian shook a fist in Court's face and roared. Court, flashing a middle finger back, stood his ground as he pedaled furiously down the road.

Court also got a glimpse of the drug culture that has long infested cycling. An ex-pro who mentored young cyclists handed Court a small foil package of what appeared to be amphetamines. "Vitamins . . . give you oomph," the ex-pro said. Court pedaled away and tossed the pills into a canal.

Yet we also found warmth and friendliness.

Teammates and I chatted with friendly Scots, although we could barely understand what they said through thick accents. We befriended a young Belgian racer, Steven Dondt of Wetteren. He led us on a memorable training ride crisscrossing the courses of the 1988 World Road Race Championship and the Tour of Flanders, including a trip up the fabled Koppenberg cobbled climb. Steven welcomed us in his house. He was from a cycling family; his brother had been a pro and competed in the Vuelta a España (Tour of Spain). His father was a soigneur, or team caretaker, with the pro Team Telekom in Germany.

Steven gave me a Tour de France water bottle . . . a memento I still have displayed in my home.

Sometimes our team, an immature bunch, simply enjoyed being on our bikes in Belgium. We rattled over cobblestones around Ghent, jumping trolley tracks and making the European siren sounds with our voices . . . "Eeee-uuuu, eeee-uuuu!" For breakfast we'd eat hard rolls, cheese, bread with chocolate spread, and strong coffee. For dinner, we'd down bowls of spaghetti.

In his letter, Court provided me with a social primer: He'd met a few fellow Americans, "pompous asses, really cocky." The Dutch guys were pretty cool, he added.

One day Court and three teammates rode along a bike path in the town of Ninove on their way to a race when a car pulled in front of them as they descended a hill. Court clipped the front of the car and was thrown over the bars; blood poured from a nasty gash in his forehead. "Jesus!" a Belgian nurse who happened by cried in English. She cared for my friend in the roadway. After a visit to the hospital, Court headed to the Eddy Merckx bicycle factory in Brussels in search of verification for insurance coverage that his bike was indeed damaged. Eddy Merckx, the greatest cyclist of all time, personally met with the young American to make the assessment.

"It's kaput!" declared Merckx, waving his arms over the bicycle.

A gritty and determined Category 1 racer, Court adapted to Belgian racing and started placing "in the money." That fall, he was invited to the US Olympic Training Center in Colorado Springs to be evaluated by US Cycling Federation coaches. Christian Vande Velde, who would go on to finish as high as fourth in the Tour de France, would be at that same camp.

Court and I would never make our livings aboard bikes. I was never close—topping out as a Category 2 racer. But a pioneering generation of Americans has used the European amateur experience as a springboard to successful pro careers.

And young Americans still keep coming to Belgium. Some come

Author hurting in 1992 kermis. Photo courtesy of Daniel Lee

by themselves or seek guidance from independent cycling centers. USA Cycling systematically sends talented young riders to Belgium as a base to race across Europe in the hope of molding young men into pros.

Teenager Lawson Craddock, a Texan, puked two times inside his mouth as he captured a silver medal at the junior world time trial championship in Moscow.

Taylor Phinney grew up the son of champions: His dad, Davis, is a two-time Tour de France stage winner, and mom Connie Carpenter-Phinney, an Olympic cycling gold medalist. He's becoming the next great hope of American cycling.

Young pro Guy East, a quiet kid from a football-playing family in Indiana, spent months in Izegem, Belgium, racing for USA Cycling's Development Team. His next step was racing on the US domestic road circuit and in six-day velodrome races in Europe.

The United States is on the leading edge of producing high-tech carbon bikes and using power meters for scientific training. But for all its modern influences, cycling at its highest level is still contested over old European roads. It requires Americans to adjust to a culture, on and off the bike, that's vastly different from their own. The Tour de France may be the pinnacle of professional cycling, but Belgium is the sport's greatest and most grueling classroom.

I was thirty-third out of sixty-six in my first Belgian race, the one with the Davy Crockett song. I didn't even officially finish—riders deemed out of contention are waved off the course in kermises. The race paid prize money thirty places deep.

I returned to dorm room 220 in Ghent and chugged warm Coke (seemingly the only sort available in Europe) from a liter bottle. "These guys attack a lot, corner slow, and accelerate fast. It's almost like a different sport from American racing," I wrote in my journal. "You can't make mistakes your first race; you just learn. And we learned a lot."

Soon I was back in the United States. I'd get engaged, start an internship and finish graduate school. But for a brief moment, I was young and part of that wild frontier.

In 1992, I competed in dozens of races in eight states and two foreign countries. In 1993, I'd get married, land my first newspaper job, and compete in zero races. I never had what it takes, yet my enthusiasm for cycling endured.

Court and I still ride, and sometimes race time trials, together. We describe Indiana's frequent cool gray weather as a perfect Belgian day for a ride. For my fortieth birthday, Court gave me a Belgian beer stein. For his fortieth, I gave Court a yellow-and-black Lion of Flanders flag, the kind waved at pro cycling races around the globe.

A new generation of Americans, though, is still hacking its way through cycling's wilderness, hoping for a shot at cycling's greatest races. And so, almost a generation after racing in Flanders, I returned to Europe—and then sampled America's domestic racing scene—to accomplish something as a writer I could never do as a rider: understand what it takes to go pro.

Navigating by Steeple

All those years ago in 1992, as a twenty-three-year-old amateur about to race in Belgium and Germany for the first time, I wrote these words in my journal: "Everything you hear about racing in Europe makes it sound like it's impossible . . . How good can they be? They're only human."

European racing was still mysterious and distant for most young Americans. TV coverage of the Tour de France back then was mostly highlight shows that featured brief race clips accompanied by melodramatic narration and synthesizer music. Without Internet sites such as CyclingNews.com, PezCyclingNews.com, and VeloNews.com and TV channels Universal Sports and Versus to provide regular race coverage, young Americans learned about races that had taken place weeks before by reading articles in *VeloNews* or *Winning* magazine. The cobbles of Paris–Roubaix and the twenty-one switchbacks of L'Alpe d'Huez were a fantasyland. Americans who ventured to Europe to race knew little of what to expect.

Yet one thing Americans realized almost instinctively was this: Racing was tougher, trickier, and faster in Europe. That was true in 1992, and it's still true today. Why? The answer is a blend of culture, history, geography, and attitude.

In seeking to prepare young Americans for top-level international racing, USA Cycling more than a decade ago set its sights on Flanders. It hired Noel Dejonckheere, and for ten years he and his wife, Els, ran what became known as the Belgian house in Izegem. It became a crucial bridge to a pro career for many high-potential US amateurs.

Steve Johnson, chief executive officer of USA Cycling, said the launch of the Belgian house marked a fundamental shift in philosophy. For decades, USA Cycling focused on preparing athletes for the Olympics. The best riders, such as Davis Phinney, would naturally go on to the pros. But starting in 1996, professional cyclists were eligible for the Olympics. In road cycling, Olympians were no longer fresh-faced amateurs. They were established stars. The strategy would have to change. Starting with inception of its Belgian-based program in 1999, USA Cycling has sought to develop riders for the highest level of professional racing—competitions such as the Tour de France and Paris–Roubaix. Americans seeing Americans succeeding in the European professional peloton is what draws new athletes into the sport, the logic goes.

USA Cycling boasts that from 1999 through early 2011, at least thirty-three riders from its development programs have been placed on teams competing in the UCI (Union Cycliste Internationale) Pro Tour or Pro Continental teams, the two highest levels of professional racing. Graduates of the program include Tour de France stage winner Dave Zabriskie and rising sprint star Tyler Farrar. In 2010, Brent Bookwalter, a graduate of the Izegem program, would finish the Giro d'Italia and the Tour de France at the age of twenty-six. Taylor Phinney was at the head of the new generation.

Yet even Phinney is not an overnight sensation. European cycling requires an extended and difficult education. USA Cycling, which spends about $500,000 a year on its men's program in Europe, predicts a roughly six- to seven-year development curve for a young rider. USA Cycling sends about 135 male and female (who are based in Italy) road racers a year to Europe. The goal is for the cyclists to compete in about sixty European races from the time they're racing in the junior category at the age of fifteen through when they turn twenty-three.

Young riders in the United States get used to driving long distances to compete in short criteriums, the multi-lap events most common in American racing. Often, junior-aged fields consist of a dozen or fewer racers. They can quickly develop a knack for the criteriums:

accelerate, corner, accelerate, corner. Savvy riders find a rhythm and strategy to sit in the slipstream until the final sprint. Even in the pros, criteriums are rarely more than fifty miles.

In Flanders, it's a much different scene: one-hundred-plus miles on small roads with two hundred riders over cobblestones, crosswinds and climbs. "In America, you could win ten criteriums and you're a hero," Dejonckheere said. "And you come here and you're a zero." Why? Europe's compact size, dense population, and tight roads breed an inherently tough brand of bike racing. Johnson said power-meter data show that it takes roughly 10 to 15 percent more output for a US national team rider to stay in a pack in a European race when compared with a US race.

In America, a cycling team could spend thousands of dollars to fly bikes and riders across the country and back for races. In Belgium, most weekends bring multiple options for racing within a few hours' drive—even if that means venturing into Holland or France. It's like finding a cornfield in Iowa.

Belgium, about the size of Maryland, hosted roughly 285 national and UCI road races in 2010, from the Tour of Flanders on down to lesser-known races such as the Triptyque Ardennais. And that number does not include the multitude of local kermis races each cycling season. The United States had just seven UCI events in 2010, with the Tour of California being the most notable. USA Cycling's National Racing Calendar offered an additional thirty high-level races. Some, such as the Tour of Utah, are stage races drawing top fields with Tour de France stars such as George Hincapie and Levi Leipheimer. Other events such as the Tour of Somerville in New Jersey and the Manhattan Beach Grand Prix have become mainstays of the US criterium circuit.

And don't forget about culture shock. It's one thing to vacation with the family in Paris or head to Brussels to buy chocolate; it's another thing to race bikes around European backstreets in a low-paying sport far from family and friends. Imagine a Dutch kid who loves basketball playing his first game of pickup hoops in Chicago.

North American amateurs heading over to Flanders tell similar stories: The racing is fast and aggressive. And if that's not enough, Belgian racers like to yell and curse at the newbie foreigners. Americans must be mentally prepared for this. If they ever want to succeed, they cannot be intimidated.

Guy East—an Indianapolis native who raced for Trek-Livestrong's U23 team in 2009 and the US-based Kelly Benefit Strategies squad in 2010—contrasted the racing styles on the two continents: In America, "You show up in Trek-Livestrong clothes and everybody just follows you around . . . Everyone is like, 'I have to show him I'm better than him.'"

And in Europe? Even at small races, the strategy is not about finding an elite rider and marking his every move. East, gripping pretend handlebars and twisting his face into an expression of pain, describes racing across the pond: "AAHHH, AAAHHHH, please slow down! Why are we going so hard?" Then, in a more serious tone, he added, "If you want to do well, you just have to be aggressive. You just have to take it into your own hands. You can't sit around and wait for things to happen."

Belgian racing also has its own form of trash talking. East told of American teammates, at first taken aback by being screamed at, starting to get into the verbal jostling themselves by screaming or even growling (yes, a loud "GGGRRRRR!") at rivals. In fact, a British website—CrazyAboutBelgium.co.uk—provides a handy list of useful phrases for English-speaking racers headed to Flanders. There are common phrases, such as *Dank U wel* for "thank you," and cycling-specific terms like *fiets* for "bike." The list also provides descriptors and phrases you won't learn in a language class: *Op kop rijden* for "ride on the front," *stomme eisel* for "stupid donkey," and *rotzak* for "bastard." The site suggests that racers print off a few of the terms and tape them to their handlebars—"natives always love it when you make the effort."

Riding at the front is crucial. But everyone knows that, so getting to the head of the peloton—where life is safer and less energy is wasted—can be a monumentally difficult task. Americans venturing to Europe are competing on roads many of their rivals have raced and trained on since they were teenagers. In America, racers jump curbs to avoid crashes. In Belgium, the curb and sidewalk are parts of the course when it comes to fighting for position.

"It's all the way down to like knowing where you can jump on the sidewalk and move up. Or knowing where you don't have to fight [for position] because in like three hundred meters it widens for a second and you can fight there, knowing when you come up around this bend out of these cobbles, you're going to have a dead crosswind" to deal with, said Jackson Stewart, a Californian riding in 2010 for the BMC Racing Team. "You get a feeling of that, and you can sense that. If you raced it two, three years in a row, you have a very good sense." Stewart compared it to the knowledge a racer gains racing lap after lap on the same circuit or criterium course: Every crack in the pavement, every stretch where it's easy to sprint up the side of the road to get to the front of the pack, is memorized.

Stewart is an accomplished cyclist. He has worn the King of the Mountains and the Most Aggressive Rider jerseys in the Tour of California. Yet the great races of Europe—Paris–Roubaix, Tour of Flanders—have proven difficult to finish. In the hard races of Holland and Belgium, Stewart looks to learn from natives such as Dutch BMC teammate Karsten Kroon, who is able to jump from the back to the front of the peloton with expertly timed bursts of speed. "I remember being with him one time, moving it up. I don't know why but I just waited with him, waited with him," Stewart said. "He's like, 'Jackson, go now, man!' We did this turn and it was wide open on the left side and we just ripped it up it like fifty spots. But he does that all day long."

USA Cycling coach and program manager Benjamin Sharp put it this way: In America, the sport often is about "racing backward." It's often a contest of attrition. The strong riders look back late in the race to find that much of the field has been whittled away. In Europe, it's all about "racing forward." Attacks are rewarded. Breakaways shred the field.

Sharp, who grew up in Indianapolis and raced in Indiana University's famed Little 500 bike race, now is building his career helping American teenagers prepare for the rigors of European racing. As USA Cycling's director of high-performance endurance, he's part camp counselor in Izegem, part parent, part friend and full-time coach.

The journey to Europe for many promising teenage cyclists starts with a review of the most basic travel tips possible. Sharp reminds teens and their parents that Belgium uses the euro for money, not the US dollar. Don't haul a bike across the Atlantic that's broken or in disrepair and expect to compete. Practice basic hygiene—having a dozen or more guys crammed into a frat-house-like setting is a breeding ground for viruses and maladies that can zap racing strength. One rider couldn't get rid of pink eye because he packed only one pair of contact lenses. The lenses spread the disease, but the kid couldn't see without them. A vicious, if preventable, cycle.

Americans obsessed with full-carbon frames and components can find their lightweight gear to be a burden in races where hopping curbs and rambling over cobbles is part of the job description. "I cringe whenever I see someone come over with the latest greatest carbon-fiber wheels or carbon bars and stem and all that stuff," Sharp said. "This is the working-class racing. You need a bike that is going be functional and not necessarily one that's going to help you go up Mont Ventoux three minutes faster."

And then there's the Belgian weather: Sharp informs new racers headed to the Izegem developmental house that Belgium averages 212 days a year with precipitation and only about fifteen hundred hours—or a precious 62 days—a year of sunshine. He straddles a delicate line in preparing young Americans for Europe: telling them what to expect and setting realistic expectations, but not over-informing or intimidating. "Our time-trial results in all levels of our sport really reflect that in the US we're breeding very strong athletes, and we're developing very strong athletes that are capable of winning time trial events. Our program is built around developing those strong engines into strong skilled engines. That's basically the cornerstone of why our program exists."

Benjamin King, front, and Cole House train on the cobbles of Flanders.
Photo by Daniel Lee

Those strong engines need fine-tuning. Elite riders should be practicing the skills they'll need in the land where cycling is a contact sport. Go out to a grassy field and practice bumping shoulders with other riders—something riders will be doing over concrete in Belgium. Practice motor pacing. In the United States, only the biggest races have caravans of cars. In Europe, many races have multiple team cars and support vehicles. A rider can't be skittish about drafting one foot off the bumper of a team car to rejoin the pack after a flat or crash. Riders should be able to bunny-hop a curb in a single bound; sometimes the sidewalk is the only way to avoid a crash or move up in the pack. Learning to eat with both hands off the handlebars while riding in a crowded pack is another must: Riders can't make it through a long road race on sports gels alone, so that means being able to grab musette feed bags and water bottles. It means being adept enough to unwrap the tinfoil around the small sweet cakes favored by European cyclists for quick energy. Be ready for anything in Europe: Sharp has seen wind gusts blow riders off their bikes and a spooked horse gallop inches from the pack. Streets are clogged with "road furniture"—roundabouts, small signs, and directional markers great for separating traffic, commuter cyclists, trams, and pedestrians but not so great for a high-speed peloton. "Road safety in America is far and above what it is in Europe. If you took [the US] pro peloton and put them into Europe, they would crap their pants and be blown away with how technical it is," said Ted King, an American who has ridden two Giros d'Italia with the Cervélo Test Team. "Basically, every day is like a six-hour crit . . . You have to be turned on mentally and physically for that time. . . . It's wild."

If a strong rider practices and learns all this, then he just might be able to do that one thing all coaches give as their top advice: Ride near the front. "Any time you're riding at the back of the pack in Europe, you're definitely in jeopardy of being dropped off the back," Sharp said. "All it takes is one rider in front of you . . . to sit up or not be able to keep up and the next thing you know you're in a group of thirty losing time to the group ahead of you of sixty."

It's known as the accordion effect. The pack of riders has a natural elasticity of expanding and contracting with changes in direction or speed during the race. But for riders at the back of the group, it's a painful reality of racing that they will be sprinting to catch up from an acceleration that the leaders have already recovered from. Those at the head of the pack are well aware of this, and don't mind exacerbating the pain for those behind them by taking narrow turns at slow speeds. "They intentionally corner badly. People think they corner badly because they don't know how to corner. They know how to corner. They're intentionally slowing down so then the guys at the back have to jump like way harder than the guys at the front," said Ian Boswell, a wispy six-foot-three, 160-pound climber from Oregon who rides with the US National Development Team.

These are hard lessons of the road. Some things riders can only understand from experience, but knowing what to expect—and being surrounded by fellow Americans who have been through the same thing—can make the transition from American criterium to European road racing less humbling and more inspiring. A simple training ride must be approached as a learning experience in a land where seemingly no road goes in a straight line. Riders learn to navigate by steeples and windmills—as the USA Cycling coaches say—to find their way from town to town and back to their rooms again. In a condensed region like Flanders, small towns are often within sight on the horizon. Remember the look of a certain church, or that Izegem is recognizable by modern windmills.

Daniel Holloway (born in 1987) told of what it was like for his friend and track-racing partner Colby Pearce (born 1972) racing twenty years ago: steel bikes, down-tube shifters, heading to Europe with no one telling him what to expect or what to do. Back then, the Europeans considered the Americans either a few freakish talents like LeMond or many clueless adventurers. "Generally, we were just labeled as dumb," Holloway said as he sat at the breakfast table in Izegem. "As a collective at their age, we're a lot smarter than those guys were."

My Davy Crockett metaphor applies here: Just as the first pioneers faced the greatest unknowns in harsh conditions in the American wilderness, Yankees who plunged themselves into Europe's road-racing scene decades ago were thrust into an unfamiliar world in which they were greeted by the locals as oddities: Guys who traveled thousands of miles to race a kermis, only to get stuck at the back of the pack struggling for two laps before being pulled from the race by the official.

In the 1970s, Missouri-native John Howard was as close as America had to a cycling star. His is the story of a remarkable career that may have been much different had Howard, born in 1947, been a generation or two younger. Howard had to find his own road in what was then a cult sport in the United States. Howard compiled an incredible résumé: an Olympian in 1968, 1972, and 1976 and winner of the Pan American Games road race in 1971. He competed in Europe, including a stage win and third place overall at the 1973 Tour of Ireland. Howard was a trailblazer of US cycling. Yet when the opportunity came to race at the sport's highest level, Howard said no: "I had many opportunities that I just let pass because I didn't have support, financial or otherwise."

Howard did get plenty of European experience. His US-based Raleigh team rode the Milk Race in Britain twice. Then Howard received an invite from the Dutch TI-Raleigh team, which in the 1970s and 1980s was a powerhouse with legendary riders including Joop Zoetemelk, Jan Raas, and Hennie Kuiper. "It would have been a domestique role, I knew that," Howard said. "But I just didn't really have the desire. It would have been in my prime, 1975–76. At that time, the Dutch riders didn't speak much English. I turned it down. I went back to school and then raced locally. In retrospect, it was a mistake. I should have done it. I would have been the first Tour de France rider from America. But you can't look back."

Howard would stay on the US National Team for ten years before being booted off to make way for younger riders despite his continued strong performances. He'd search and find extreme cycling challenges: setting the bicycle-speed record by riding 152.2 miles per hour on the Bonneville Salt Flats in 1985 and the world twenty-four-hour cycling distance record of 593 miles in 1987.

Yet while those feats gained Howard notoriety, the attention of America's cycling fans—what few there were—was turning toward

Europe. In 1985, Greg LeMond finished second in the Tour de France after famously being ordered by his French team to wait for faltering French teammate Bernard Hinault on the mountain stage to Luz Ardiden. LeMond, in front with Irishman Stephen Roche, was on pace to take the yellow jersey. LeMond would go on to win the time trial at Lac de Vassiviere that year, becoming the first American to win a stage at the Tour. In 1986, LeMond's rivalry with Hinault would boil over into a team feud as the American sought his first Tour win and the Frenchman his sixth. But LeMond would triumph to win his first Tour de France.

Even in 1987, as LeMond recovered from a near-fatal shotgun wound in a hunting accident that spring, Americans made news at the Tour de France. Team 7-Eleven's Davis Phinney won stage 12 into Bordeaux and teammate Jeff Pierce won the final stage in Paris. By the 1980s, US cycling had made the leap from an underground sport to one with Tour de France credentials.

Inspired American amateurs increasingly were Belgium-bound. Glenn Hays was like many racers back then—he met a guy who raced bikes, initially thought the guy was nuts for training fifty miles a day, but then was intrigued enough to take up the sport himself. After Hays got out of the Navy, where he had met his cycling mentor, he moved to Long Beach, California, and started racing. During the 1984 Los Angeles Summer Olympics, he rode to and watched the team time trial along Artesia Freeway (where Americans Davis Phinney, Ron Kiefel, Roy Knickman, and Andrew Weaver took bronze) and the road race in Mission Viejo (where American Alexi Grewal took gold). Hays wanted to be like them.

By 1987, the twenty-five-year-old Hays was racing on the Raleigh team. He ended up going to Belgium that season with teenage teammate Dominic Felde at the urging of coach Greg Miller, who himself had raced in Flanders years before. "Raleigh liked the idea and gave us a few things and a little money that ran out quickly, so we pretty much paid for it ourselves," Hays said.

Miller, with his Belgian connections, helped set the pair up with an apartment—it was a place to live, even if it ranked below college rental house standards. Hays remembered his Belgian landlord: "Nice old lady in a huge elegant house right across the street from our shitty, no-way-up-to-code flat we lived in." For starters, the flat was on the fourth floor and the bathroom on the ground floor. No refrigerator. No shower, which meant Hays took sponge baths. Only cold water flowed from the tap. And that water had to be boiled first to ensure it was drinkable. The water was heated on the stove for sponge baths. Milk and potato soup were placed on the ledge in the cool Belgian night air to prevent them from spoiling. With stores closing early in Ghent, food shopping had to be done by 5 PM—tough on race days—or the pair would be stuck eating greasy sausages and *frites* from a tavern. "Sometimes we would walk over to the university cafeteria and act like students so we could eat for free," said Hays, who got a job tinting windows on new BMWs to survive.

If the accommodations were Stone Age in harshness, so was the racing. Hays, a lean five-eleven and 145 pounds, was a climber looking to help Felde, a sprinter, over flat windswept courses. Felde scored a few top-five results, but highlights for Hays were few. He attacked early in one road race passing over some of the same climbs used in the Liege–Bastogne–Liege Spring Classic. His aggression was rewarded with a spot in a fourteen-man breakaway—he hung on to finish fourteenth. "I guess that was my best result," he said.

The process of turning in the reusable number to the local tavern after the race could be just as forbidding as the competition. Thrashed from the race, Hays wandered through tavern air rank from hours of cigar smoking by overweight and sometimes unshowered Belgian men who had gathered to see the race. Being an American cyclist in Belgium, though, did have some benefits. Hays didn't have a girlfriend back home, but realized that in Belgium being a bike racer could boost his status with women. Ghent, a university town, had plenty of nightlife. And Hays gladly took part in it. "Once you tell girls that you are an American bike racer, it's all good," he said. For a time he dated a woman who lived north of Ghent in Holland— visits also were a chance to enjoy a shower and clean water.

In 1990, three years after his stint in Ghent, a waterskiing accident left Hays unable to walk for six months. By that time, he had raced in Europe, in Australia, and across the United States—and he knew he didn't have what it took to be a top pro. He had returned to South- ern California to work in the music industry, recording albums and touring as a bass player with the FleshEaters and other alternative music acts. He worked as a DJ in Amsterdam for a few years. In 2005 and 2006, he played shows in Ghent and in the Flemish town of Oudenaarde. He looked at the young people at those shows and re- alized, "The year they were born, I was entertaining their parents by racing my bike; eighteen years later, I'm entertaining kids, playing records." In 2010, Hays was back in Southern California racing his bike in masters events and working in the music industry, including as a voting member of the Recording Academy for the Grammy Awards. Yet he still thinks often about Belgium. "I still have an ad- diction to going back to that part of the world."

Belgium, though, is now territory to be explored by the next gen- eration of Americans. On a chilly late-March day, US National De- velopment Team riders Cole House, Ian Boswell, Benjamin King, and Andrew Barker pedaled away from Izegem for a training ride and team photo shoot. Within an hour of leaving their team house, they ended up on the steep slopes of the Paterberg, one of the climbs used in the Tour of Flanders. Andrew Hawkes, European program manager for USA Cycling, drove the accompanying Audi Team USA car, with photographer Casey Gibson snapping publicity photos along the way. Next, they headed to the cobbled Oude Kwaremont climb for more photos. The young Americans wrestled their bikes from side to side over the old stones. Sweating even in the chilled air, they stopped at the top of the famous cobbled climb to shed their thermal vests and grab an energy gel from Hawkes.

"You want a quote for your book?" asked young American Ian Boswell. "Cobblestones are stupid." The others laughed and joined in what was obviously a running joke: Stone by stone, a cobblestone path was the hardest way possible to build a road. At first the cobblestones are greeted with excitement by the young Americans. Then, after many bone-jarring passages, they simply become a tough part of an already tough sport. House then took the light moment in another direction. "Yeah, we stop for some coffee?" House suggested to his teammates in a wonderfully fake Flemish accent. The Americans were far from home, yes, but even in their bright red, white, and blue US team colors, they blended into the drab Belgian day.

3

Grim Beauty

Almost eighteen years had passed since my own short trip to Belgium to race bikes. Back then, I was a graduate student figuring out the world and my place in it. I returned to Belgium as a forty-one-year-old husband and father creeping into middle age. I was still thin, especially by modern American standards, but each day seemed to bring a new fleck of gray hair around my temples. In writing this book, I tried to view the American racers I'd meet—some of them young enough to be my kids—with the objective eye of a reporter. But I also found myself looking at many of them with the feelings of affection and worry that come with growing older and experiencing more of life's joys and hurts.

It was just after 7 AM on a depressingly gray Saturday in early April as I made the short walk from my rented room just off the central square in Izegem to the house of USA Cycling's National Development Team near the edge of town.

Kortrijksestraat, the residential street the plain red-brick home is situated along, was empty of cars, bikes, and pedestrians. Even the nearby bakery—which provides daily bread and the occasional pastry for the US national team riders—had not yet opened.

For the moment, all was quiet. But this would be an epic day. In fact, USA Cycling transformed this boxy aging home into its Belgian training base so promising young American riders could experience days just like this.

Inside the Izegem house, cyclists prepared for day two of le Triptyque des Monts et Châteaux—one of the US national team's key European races during the 2010 spring season.

Cole House—who trained alone on narrow Flemish roads in order to memorize them, because those routes also are racecourses—looked to be almost sleepwalking as he shuffled out of the kitchen clutching a cup of coffee. Others such as sprinter Daniel Holloway were in search of clothes or equipment. This was the calm beginning to a long, tense, and dangerous day. Some of his teammates were still in bed. Others already had headed out for the roughly hour-and-a-half drive to Lessines, the town in the French-speaking portion of Belgium that would host that morning's 8.4-kilometer individual time trial. A road race would follow in the afternoon, a contest in which House and Holloway would play key roles.

Le Triptyque des Monts et Châteaux is a three-day Belgian stage race totaling 477.3 kilometers (297 miles), made up of three road races and a short time trial. It's for developing young riders—those vying to be the next generation of pro cycling stars and domestiques. The course wound through small towns and cities and lush green rolling countryside.

The Americans, led by Taylor Phinney, had showed their strength on Friday's stage 1, a 170.2-kilometer (106-mile) mostly flat but winding route from Vieux-Condé, in France, to Quevaucamps, in Belgium.

"Last year after this race I wrote in my training diary 'win this race next year.' Guess what? It's next year," Phinney posted on his Twitter account that day.

He was off to an impressive start on the race's first day. The field of 153 riders would be split apart by strong crosswinds on the blustery Northern European spring day. US teammates House, Holloway, and Gavin Mannion rode near Phinney, making sure he made the front group. With only about five kilometers to go, Phinney would suffer a flat tire, but he managed to catch back onto the front pack with just two kilometers to go.

Still, though, this was Phinney—who, even though he was only nineteen at the time, was the reigning world pursuit champion. He was one of the fastest finishers of any age over a race's last few kilometers. Phinney sprinted to fourth place behind Frederique Robert of Belgium and Dutchmen Wippert Woulter and Jetse Bol.

"Nutted up," Phinney said via Twitter.

The other Americans, the ones who helped pace Phinney, would finish farther down: House in fifty-fourth place, Holloway in fifty-eighth, and Mannion in ninety-first were in the front group with him—a group that averaged 26.75 miles per hour for 106 miles. American Benjamin King, a serious student who left his studies at Virginia Tech to pursue cycling full-time, was among the riders to finish more than fourteen minutes behind Phinney's group.

King was caught in a crash—one of bike racing's endless and dangerous chain-reaction wrecks—just eighteen miles into the stage. In the tangle of bodies and bikes, the sharp teeth of another rider's chainring ripped into King's left leg just below the knee. He remounted and pedaled the day's remaining eighty-seven miles with a mud-smeared gash that stretched across the front of his leg. After the race, King looked down to see a congealed cranberry-sauce-like mixture of blood and mud seeping from his wound. The jagged wound would take nine stitches to close and would end King's race.

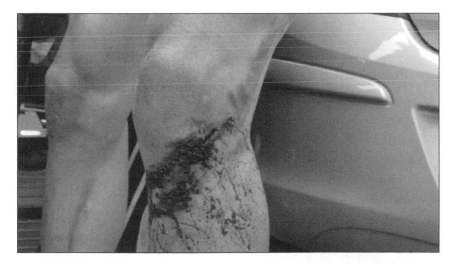

A deep gash from a crash ended Benjamin King's race, though he finished the day's stage with the wound. Photo courtesy of Benjamin King

Triptyque des Monts et Châteaux would bring more injury, drama, and exhilaration for the young Americans.

Day 2, on Saturday, would begin with an 8.4-kilometer individual time trial in the Belgian hamlet of Lessines and end in the afternoon with a 134.4-kilometer road race from Frasnes-lez-Buissenal to Soignies, Belgium. A strong performance in the morning time trial would be crucial to Phinney's goal of winning the three-day race. He started the second day in ninth place, ten seconds behind overall leader Frederique Robert of Belgium.

The time trial began at 9 AM Saturday, with one rider starting off every minute. Each cyclist would ride alone—one man against the clock. Stage races, especially ones not traversing large mountains, often are won in the time trial. (In the first stage, 97 of the 141 finishers completed the race in the same time.)

So this much was clear: This race would come down to seconds.

Phinney was in perfect position to go for the win. His fourth-place finish in stage 1 meant he would be one of the final riders to start the time trial. (In stage races, riders start time trials in reverse order of their standing, meaning the top riders go last.) That meant he could sleep a little later, scout the course, and have a good idea of what time he would need to win.

The triangle-shaped course started and finished on a straight blacktop street with cobblestone sidewalks. On either side of the street, the Chaussée Gabrielle Richet, ran a neat row of narrow shops and houses. Team buses, vans, and cars were parked on both sides of the road. Team tents, cycling's version of locker rooms, provided shelter from the intermittent rain for riders as they warmed up on turbo trainers.

Casey Gibson, USA Cycling's photographer, and I headed to the start line to get our media credentials. After several inquiries, we were directed from the beer tent to a small camper parked near the starting ramp. Gibson knocked; no answer. Another knock; again no answer. He then grabbed the door handle and tried to enter—which brought a gruff stream of what had to be French obscenities. I joked that, based on the anger and urgency in his voice, he must have been sitting on the camper's toilet.

We finally figured out we were a bit early. A few minutes later, we would return to find the camper's window open. A large, almost rotund, elderly man gave us the race roster and program as well as our press passes without even asking who we were or what organization we represented.

It was a quick example of navigating life in a foreign nation: Even simple tasks come with a bit more confusion and stress. Just the day before I had missed a scheduled phone interview with Team Garmin-Transitions director Jonathan Vaughters after a broken train partway between Ghent and Izegem had me frantically trying to figure out how to catch the last connection back to my bed-and-breakfast room. For cyclists, such small off-the-bike stuff accumulates to zap away precious bits of energy.

After stopping in a bakery along the course for a quick coffee and pastry, I headed back to the Development Team's tent along the finishing stretch. Riders sprinted by as they finished the time trial at the same time others warmed up and spectators crossed the street. It seemed chaotic and dangerous, yet the riders whizzed by without incident. USA Cycling officials said the federation's insurance representative would never tolerate such a potentially dangerous scene.

Despite all of the activity around him, Phinney was serious and focused. Dressed in a hoodie sweatshirt to guard against the morning chill, Phinney climbed into the front seat of the USA Cycling team car that would follow teammate Gavin Mannion as he navigated the time trial course. I climbed in the backseat to also ride along.

Mannion rolled down the green start house ramp and briefly sprinted before settling into his aerodynamic tuck. Belgian Chris Lefevere, director of Team USA for this race, quickly pulled up behind him in the team's following car. Mannion started under heavily cloudy skies with some rain. One of the trickiest parts of the course came just a few hundred meters after the start—a sharp right-hand bend through a small roundabout where the rider enters at seven o'clock and exits at four o'clock. Despite the wet roads, a top placing depended on keeping speed high, because coming out of this turn was a slight uphill.

Taylor Phinney warms up his big engine. Photo by Daniel Lee

"Holy shit," Phinney exclaimed as the car skidded through the turn, losing a bit of ground to Mannion before accelerating back up to him. "Go! Go! Go!" Lefevere yelled to Mannion out the driver's-side window. "Good job! Go!"

Mannion rose out of the saddle and sprinted up the brief uphill section before settling into his aerodynamic tuck, his arms extended before him like a human praying mantis. Much of the course was over twelve-foot-wide concrete roads. Despite the rain and chilly temperatures of about forty-five degrees, Mannion looked comfortable as he kept his speed between twenty-five and thirty-five miles an hour most of the way. Phinney watched from the passenger seat in silence as Mannion screamed through the downhill portion of the course, hitting thirty-six miles per hour in spots and gliding over three sets of railroad tracks. Mannion crossed the finish line with a time of 11:03—a solid time that should place him in the top twenty.

Phinney now could visualize the course, and his victory on it. He headed back to where Team USA's team truck was parked several hundred yards up from the finish line to begin the pre-time-trial ritual. He stripped down to his stars-and-stripes USA skinsuit and leaned against the truck as one of the team helpers carefully affixed the number 66 to the middle of his lower back. He headed into the team tent and climbed aboard his Trek time trial bike to warm up on the turbo trainer. Phinney, wearing headphones, looked focused as he whirled the pedals on his carbon-fiber Trek machine.

Soon he zipped up his skinsuit and put on his aero helmet and warm-up jacket—which would be discarded shortly before he raced—and headed to the start house.

He waited in silence with other riders. One by one they headed to the start ramp, mounted their carbon-fiber time trial bikes, and awaited the race official's final countdown in French.

"Cinq, quatre, trois, deux, un!"

Julien Paquet of Belgium sprinted away. A minute later, Marcel Kittel of Germany began his race. Phinney was next: He had seen the course, had seen teammate Mannion post a top time. This was Phinney's chance to put himself into the yellow leader's jersey of the Triptyque des Monts et Châteaux.

Phinney rolled down the ramp and was soon up to speed. He navigated the sharp right-hand bend through the roundabout and was quickly back in his full aerodynamic tuck as he whooshed by me over wet roads. The Team USA car, driven by Chris Lefevere, pulled in behind Phinney. In the backseat rode teammate Daniel Holloway, who had just minutes before finished his run to post an impressive time of 11:02.

Holloway—who at age twenty-two was a veteran of USA Cycling's Development Team program in Belgium—seemed to draw energy from being around and racing with the teenage-prodigy Phinney. Holloway appreciated, even admired, the teenager's confident and positive attitude. And Phinney seemed to benefit from the presence of Holloway, a savvy racer who had become an elder statesmen on the US squad.

Phinney was on form. His long torso rocked methodically as he churned his pedals to power his Trek along at more than thirty miles an hour. The day and the landscape were unmistakably spring in Belgium: Concrete-slab streets laid out in sections, leaving a thick gap that ran down the center of the road. It was a common hazard, a rut that could catch a bicycle tire and cause a crash. Red-brick homes dotted the course. Deep drainage ditches ran alongside the road for much of the course. Green fields and tall leafless trees loomed on the horizon as Phinney motored on.

As he passed the midway point in the time trial, Phinney already was thirty seconds ahead of teammate Mannion's time—this was a race-winning time. Yet to go that fast, Phinney was teetering on the edge of control.

"Come on, Taylor! Best time!" Lefevere yelled as he drove the team car. "Go! Go!" He had to yell: No radios were allowed in this race.

Holloway also was excited and nervous. He had just ridden this same course and knew it held many dangers.

"Oh, no!" Holloway gasped from the backseat as Phinney took a corner so fast that he nearly snagged his skinsuit on the red bricks of a house sitting on the edge of the street.

"Good job, buddy! Good job!" Holloway said as Phinney accelerated out of the corner safely.

I had watched Phinney round the first corner and power up the short hill. I then walked the course backward to where the Team USA tent was set up a few hundred meters from the finish in anticipation of seeing Phinney streak by in the next few minutes.

Meanwhile Phinney still was riding on the brink with only a little more than two kilometers to go. He had safely navigated a slick set of railroad tracks and a sweeping right turn where he came uncomfortably close to the steel barricades.

Now Phinney turned left onto a flat but wet stretch of road approaching a sharp right turn.

"It's slick here, bud," said Holloway, speaking to Phinney even though his friend could not hear him. Holloway's voice was tense. He knew Phinney was approaching a particularly dangerous and sharp right turn.

"Get out of your aerobars, bud," said Holloway, wanting Phinney to position his hands near the brakes so he had more control as he rounded the corner. Phinney stayed in his aero tuck. Holloway's voice grew more tense as he yelled repeatedly:

"Get out of your bars!

"Get out of your bars!

"Get out of your bars!"

Phinney would rise from his aerobars just before the corner. But it was too late. He had too much speed headed into the corner, which left him headed straight for the metal barricades separating the course from traffic in the other lane.

"Oh, my God!" Holloway yelled.

Phinney slid to the ground and under the barricade to narrowly miss a red minivan that had just driven by in the other lane. Holloway, Lefevere, and another team staff member jumped from the car and grabbed a spare bike from the roof rack. Phinney was already back up on his feet, waiting for a bike. He jumped on the standard road bike—no aerobars, no rear carbon disc wheel—and pedaled away.

In an instant, Phinney lost the time trial and experienced a scary fall. Back on the homestretch, I watched Phinney approach and pass by on his spare bike. I knew something had happened. I hoped it was a simple flat tire.

Phinney finished and returned to the Team USA tent. He unzipped his skinsuit, draped his sweatshirt over his bare chest, and sat on an orange cooler to examine his injuries—which included a banged-up right knee.

Dutch rider Jetse Bol of the Rabobank Continental team would win the morning time trial with a time of 10:45 for the 8.4 kilometers. That placed him in the race leader's yellow jersey, with a nine-second edge over Dutch teammate Wilco Kelderman.

Among the Americans, Mannion—the rider Phinney had watched navigate the course before him—was sixteenth with a time eighteen seconds slower than Bol's. Holloway, who had nervously watch Phinney push himself beyond control, was seventeen seconds back in fourteenth. Phinney, despite his crash and bike change, was seventh—fourteen seconds slower than Bol.

What if? Consider the mid-race report that Phinney was thirty seconds quicker than teammate Mannion. Does that mean Phinney would have beat Bol by twelve seconds and taken the yellow jersey? What if longtime USA Cycling Development Team coach Noel Dejonckheere, who had left the program that season to join the pro BMC Team, had been in the car yelling detailed instructions about the course to Phinney? Dejonckheere was famous for his ability to read a race.

There was little time to think about such things. The race ambulance pulled up to the Team USA tent to offer Phinney assistance. Soon the race entourage would move to Frasnes-lez-Buissenal for the start of stage 2B, a 134.2-kilometer rolling road race through Belgian countryside scheduled for that afternoon.

American Cole House, who had finished the time trial fifty seconds back in seventy-third place, remarked that this would be a long day. But House, as he pointed at a long-haired beautiful young woman, said looking at the "scenery" could help pass some time.

"The real race," he remarked, "is this afternoon."

Fluffy white clouds rolled across the sky revealing glimpses of warming springtime sun as the 2:50 PM start of the afternoon road race, stage 2B, approached. Riders pedaled around backstreets toward the cobblestone square of the village hosting the race's start.

Riders stopped by the tent to sign in for the stage. Middle-aged men drank beer from plastic cups as they watched racers gather at the start line. One racer very indiscreetly urinated into a pot of lovely yellow flowers. Public peeing by riders seems to be highly tolerated at bike races in Europe. This is perhaps a realization by fans that cyclists keep themselves well hydrated and simply need to go. In America, such behavior would bring rebuke from race officials and complaints by residents of wherever the race was being held.

I was spending the day with Andrea Smith, USA Cycling's communications director, and photographer Casey Gibson. With Gibson behind the wheel of the rented car, we drove to the countryside outside of the Belgian town of Ath to wait for the passing peloton. Gibson, scouting for picturesque backdrops for photos, chose a tree-lined country road surrounded by pastures and freshly plowed fields. The sun and blue sky were gone now. Rain fell intermittently, making it chilly enough to at times put my rain jacket on over my thick hooded sweatshirt.

A European bike race is a rolling and well-ordered sequence of marketing and sporting traditions. First, the race's publicity caravan,

A miserable day in the rain. Photo by Daniel Lee

a parade of sponsor vehicles, crept into view. The passengers inside tossed freebies to us roadside as they whizzed by: I grabbed a reusable grocery bag for my wife and a French-language coloring and activity book for my kids.

Then I heard the sound that, as Belgian cycling fans know, means the race is near: the singing Rodania car. The Swiss watchmaker sponsors the car famous for warning those roadside the riders are approaching. The car's roof is outfitted with a large sign that says COURSE, two large megaphones, and a triangular red caution sign declaring "!". The two megaphones blurt out an unending audio-branding campaign: a four-beat trumpet intro of "Ba, ba, ba, baaa" followed by a male voice signing "RO-DAN-EE-AH, RO-DAN-EE-AH!" over and over again.

Soon I saw a four-man breakaway approaching, including one rider in stars and stripes. Cole House. He pedaled by in a group that appeared to be working well together, trading pulls into the bone-chilling wind. House's aggressiveness would help his team—riders such as Phinney and Holloway, with their teammate in the breakaway, could stay out of the wind and leave the pacesetting to teams such as Rabobank.

A couple of minutes later, the peloton approached. One rider veered off the right side of the road and somersaulted into the rain-soaked muddy field. The pack fanned across the road with Rabobank riders at the front setting the pace for race leader Bol. Then, near the rear of the field, I saw Taylor Phinney. He drifted to the right side of the road and prepared to pull down the front of his bibs to pee. His right knee was bandaged. He looked miserable. I wondered to myself if he'd even finish the stage. That thought quickly passed from my head as I watched the rider I'd just seen take a tumble—his backside covered in mud—surfing his way through the team vehicles in an attempt to rejoin the pack. The scene reminded me of the many photos I'd seen in cycling magazines over the years of mud-covered racers in Belgium.

Gibson remarked that most of the riders were wearing shorts on a day when the temperatures lingered in the forties. Some even had short sleeves. The pros would be bundled up, Gibson said. He attributed the underdressing of the young racers to a bit of machismo. Holloway, after the race, confirmed that: "In Belgium, you know, everyone wants to be a tough guy. Wear no gloves, no arm warmers, stuff like that."

The race had started off in chilly dry conditions but quickly deteriorated to a cold wet slog as stage 2B entered its final kilometers. Later Gibson scouted out a sweeping bend as a good spot to snap some pictures. The riders would pass through here twice on a finishing circuit before ending in the town of Soignies. A stretch of concrete road ran from a distant forest over rolling open countryside before winding around the estate where we were parked. Before the riders approached, Gibson and Andrea Smith left our position on the bend to walk a couple of hundred yards along the large brick fence to where the course made a left-hand turn. But a stiff wind greeted them as they made the turn and left the protective barrier of the fence.

"Just bitter," Gibson said of the wind when he returned to our spot. He then ventured into a grassy field to shoot photos of the approaching riders.

The peloton pedaled by at a good clip—probably twenty-six miles an hour—the riders looking tired and worn. We scanned the field for Team USA kits. There was Holloway, who also saw us: "Hi, Andrea," he called out from the pack in a flirty way. We watched a breakaway with a slight advantage followed by the pack pass through the spot for the second and last time before heading to the finish. A chaotic mass field sprint seemed inevitable.

Smith was not the only one Holloway was talking to as the stage neared its end. Holloway also was talking up his buddy, Taylor Phinney. Holloway would say afterward that he knew Phinney had been shaken by his crash in the morning time trial. And Holloway also knew that the final kilometers of Saturday afternoon's road race would be dangerous, especially with the roads slick from rain. "It was narrow. It was technical where you didn't have an out. It was tight with buildings," Holloway said. "So if you went down, you were going to hit a wall. There was no grass or anything."

Indeed, brick homes came right up to the street's edge on the last couple of corners that would decide the race. As those hazards approached, Holloway rode alongside his friend. "This morning was a joke," he told Phinney, referring to the crash. "It shouldn't have happened, but it did. That shouldn't change your outlook."

Holloway said he knew Phinney was the fastest in the world over a kilometer or two—Phinney's world individual pursuit championship just days before on the track had proven that. Near the end of the race, Holloway rode to the front of the pack and launched an attack. He was brought back. Then US teammate Gavin Mannion countered with his own short-lived breakaway. Race leader Jetse Bol was right there.

I stood, soaked and cold in the driving rain, on the edge of the street just past the finish line. The race commentary was in French, so we could understand only the riders' names . . . Mannion, Phinney. A thin bearded man standing next to me, recognizing that I was an American, commented on Phinney being a future star of pro cycling. The man was from Izegem—the European home of the US Development Team. I nodded and reminded him that Phinney's father, Davis, had won Tour de France stages.

Meanwhile Phinney took the lead approaching the final turns. He had a small gap. Holloway followed as the second rider, making it more difficult for Bol and the others to catch up to Phinney, who was already accelerating away from the pack. Bol and others passed by Holloway in pursuit of the young American, but it was too late. Phinney pumped his bike up the final rise and into view of the finishing straight lined with umbrella-carrying fans. Rain fell as hard as it had all day when Phinney spread his arms wide in victory. Holloway, back among the sprinting field, took the extra time to raise his own arms in celebration.

Taylor Phinney wins and Daniel Holloway celebrates.
Photo by www.cycling-pics.be

"It was funny to watch because I was ten guys back just watching guys try to drag-race Taylor on a wide-open road," Holloway said. "It just shows what kind of rider Taylor is when you pick that kid up when he has a bad day; that's what he is going to do day in and day out. That kid is a freak."

Freak, indeed. As I watched Jetse Bol sprint in two seconds behind Phinney's time of 3:18:21 for second place with what remained of the pack, I was struck by just how anguished the riders looked. Mannion rolled in 44th place, House in 101st. Soaked and exposed for hours to cold conditions, many racers had to be close to hypothermia. I watched as some, their faces masks of misery, trailed in minutes behind Phinney. For a moment, as I stood there freezing with a pounding headache, bike racing to me seemed an unreasonably harsh—even unhealthy—sport. I watched as Phinney walked across the stage to accept the winner's bouquet from a well-bundled podium girl and a man with an exquisite handlebar mustache. Phinney had to politely tell the race announcer requesting an interview that he did not speak French. I had to think that one day he would.

The victory moved Phinney into third place overall, fourteen seconds behind Dutchman Bol. And Phinney would show his power and panache on Sunday during the final stage of the Triptyque des Monts et Châteaux. This stage would be the toughest of the race: a 102-mile race that included at least ten climbs. Phinney again would be in position for the victory but would pull a foot out of his pedal in the final sprint to finish second to Belgian Edward Theuns. Bol was third, sealing his overall victory twelve seconds ahead of Phinney. Holloway, in twentieth place 1:02 behind the winner, was the only other American to complete the three-day race. The race was so tough that only 79 of the 153 starters would finish.

After watching Phinney win his stage Saturday, Casey Gibson, Andrea Smith, and I drove northwest from Soignies, in French-speaking Belgium, back to Izegem, in Dutch-speaking Flanders. The rain that had pelted the riders throughout the day stopped, and sun glowed from behind misty clouds. Throughout the day, the only times it rained were when the riders were on their bikes. The day had been a showcase for the grim beauty of cycling: a sport where riders must go to the edge, but not beyond. Young American Benjamin King had sliced his knee and was unable to continue. Phinney had pushed it too far in the time trial and lost his chance for overall victory with his crash. Yet just hours later, Holloway and Phinney would navigate dangerous wet turns to perfection for a dramatic stage win, all against a top international field. Races like this don't exist in America. Days like this prepare young Americans for the Spring Classics, for Grand Tours, in a way US criteriums simply cannot.

We looked out the right side of the car and saw a brilliant rainbow, arching down from the sky into the fertile green Belgian farmland. The day's harsh rain had, indeed, created something beautiful.

Taylor and Tyler

Taylor Phinney, sporting a tracksuit and sunglasses, led a group of teammates into the De Leest Community Center's auditorium in Izegem. He took one glance at the empty stage, illuminated by warm, bright spotlights, and declared: "This is where I belong." Phinney, then still a teenager, already had the swagger of a champion.

This dreary Belgian spring day was team photo day for USA Cycling's 2010 National Development Team. Phinney enjoyed the attention that came with being America's next great cycling hope. He and his skinny teammates—all riders under the age of twenty-three—stripped out of their warm-ups to reveal their lean limbs and stars-and-stripes-covered Team USA cycling kits. Cycling shoes clicked as they climbed onto the stage.

USA Cycling photographer Casey Gibson is used to squatting in ditches and climbing mountainsides to snap photos of bike races in wind, rain, or summer heat. Now his job was perhaps tougher: Get a bunch of college-aged guys to cooperate during a task that seems tailor- (or Taylor-) made for goofing off. Sprinter Daniel Holloway, a red-haired California kid who wore garish black-framed eyeglasses and went by the nickname "Hollywood," strutted in late wearing last year's jersey. But Phinney, at six-foot-four, stood out the most amid his teammates—jokes just seem funnier when they come from a world champion.

Gibson looked over the eight riders gathered on the stage to find Phinney towering above the rest. "Taylor, you're just a tad too tall," he said. Taylor slouched down to take six inches off his height before moving off the back riser. Now Gibson had to get the proper facial expressions. "A serious look but not angry," he requested. Phinney stared ahead in a tense stone-faced gaze that was more ridiculous than serious before breaking into a laugh. Wisconsin native Cole House cracked up at the same time. The horseplay was a reminder that these riders were still maturing—as men, as athletes. Finally, the riders' positions and expressions were acceptable, and Gibson snapped his final shots of the team.

Afterward, Phinney stretched his long frame on the stage as the women of Team USA prepared for their photos. An almost unlimited potential of cycling stardom was pent up inside his muscular legs, stretched across the stage floor. The year was young, but the season already was well under way for the then-nineteen-year-old Phinney. And the early results confirmed his status as America's latest cycling prodigy. The next LeMond? The next Armstrong? Better yet, the first Taylor Phinney—a new star for a new generation.

In February, Phinney sprinted to two top-ten stage finishes in the Tour of Qatar. The weeklong Middle Eastern race is an early season form-checker for top pros such as Tom Boonen and Heinrich Haussler as they prepare for another long season ahead . . . Milan–San Remo, Tour of Flanders, Paris–Roubaix, the Tour de France. For Phinney, it was an introduction to big-time racing. "Get a little elbowy with some of the big pros," as Phinney described it.

He saw himself developing into a rider like Boonen, or perhaps Swiss star Fabian Cancellara—powerful athletes who excel in sprints or one-day events such as the cobblestone classics of Tour of Flanders and Paris–Roubaix.

Even with Phinney's power and talent, the step up to top-level racing is an adjustment. He knew that in the sprints in Qatar, he'd lacked that final kick: "The last five minutes of races like that are really high power and it's similar to doing a pursuit," he said. "I have that ability to hold that power for four or five minutes. It's just then ramping it up at the end for the final sprint that I'm missing a little bit."

Phinney's ascension to big-time cycling was itself a sign America had developed a lineage and heritage in professional cycling that did not exist a generation ago. Longtime US cycling fans can look at his boyish face and lanky-but-developed body and see what appears to be a perfect fifty–fifty genetic and physical split between his mom and dad: the thin features and frame of his mother, 1984 Olympic road race gold medalist Connie Carpenter-Phinney, and the muscular beach-body physique of his father, two-time Tour de France stage winner Davis Phinney. "My mom was an all-rounder. She could climb; she could time trial," he said. "But I have the power and speed of my dad."

Initially, Phinney didn't even have an interest in cycling. Soccer was his sport. Or simply running and jumping off things. As a youngster, he lived in Italy where his parents ran a cycling camp and learned to cope with his father's early-onset Parkinson's disease. Then in 2005, he and his dad were at the Tour de France and met with Lance Armstrong and Axel Merckx, Belgian pro and son of cycling legend Eddy Merckx. Once Phinney switched to cycling, success came quickly. In 2006, he posted a second place in USA Cycling's junior national time trial. The next year, he was world time trial champ. In 2008 came a batch of elite national track championships—rare for a teenager competing against grown men—and a seventh place in the individual pursuit track cycling event at the Beijing Olympics.

He knows his own talent. "For some people it takes a longer time to get used to racing with the Europeans and just the different style . . . For me it sort of just clicked. I have the cycling genes in my blood, so that might help a little bit," Phinney added with deadpan humor.

Phinney tells of his dad—a member of the 7-Eleven team that was, in 1986, the first US squad to compete in the Tour de France—coming to Europe in the 1980s, being stuck in some tiny room with no TV and left to read the same book over and over. Davis would go on to become the first American to win a road-race stage of the Tour de France. He racked up 328 career victories, most of them in the 1980s before Taylor was born.

I mention to Taylor how, more than twenty years ago, I had a magazine poster of his father hanging on my bedroom wall. "He was probably wearing some big glasses. He had a yellow headband on or something, his long flowing hair," Phinney said, letting out a slight droll laugh at the end. Yes, Taylor, that pretty much summed up my circa-1988 Davis Phinney magazine poster.

Greg LeMond was the undisputed star of US cycling in the 1980s. But LeMond rode for European teams through his rise to win the 1986 Tour, his recovery from the near-fatal hunting accident in 1987, and his two later Tour wins. His eight-second victory in the 1989 Tour de France over Frenchman Laurent Fignon remains one of the most dramatic moments in sports history. But a true cycling nation needs more than one hero, and this is where Davis Phinney came in. He was a daring, handsome sprinter who, at least sometimes, beat the Europeans at their own dangerous game. He could win a Tour de France stage into Bordeaux, and then come back home and win a fifty-mile criterium.

For American teenagers interested in cycling but raised on football and baseball, Davis just seemed like an athlete—he had a star quarterback's smile and bulging biceps in a sport known for riders' twig-like arms. Davis ended his career in the early 1990s riding for the domestic Coors Light team—by then he was in his thirties, and his sprint was diminished. But he provided some needed star power on the US racing circuit.

No doubt, Taylor Phinney comes from US cycling royalty. But when I first arrived at USA Cycling's team house in Izegem, the world champ was buzzing around doing household chores. He carried a laundry basket to the washing machine. He grabbed a scrub brush and tackled his breakfast dishes. House rules demand such domestic duties, although the place is perpetually messy. Phinney then settled back into a seat at the long dining table in the main room to talk with me. Sprinter Daniel Holloway, still eating his morning cereal, sat across from me and next to Phinney.

Daniel Holloway and Taylor Phinney at breakfast in Izegem.
Photo by Daniel Lee

Topics of conversation can switch quickly for well-traveled guys of this age. For a moment, it was women. I had asked about the difficulty in keeping a steady girlfriend given that elite cyclists spend months away from home. "I don't stay away from girls. I try to stay away from settling down, at least for now," Phinney said. Then the focus drifted to observations of the female racers they see at international competitions.

Holloway: "Italy generally has better girls."

Phinney: "There's a cute Polish girl."

Holloway: "There's almost one from every nation."

Phinney: "There's a cute Belgian girl."

The sacrifices to make it as a pro are significant, even for someone of Phinney's talent. College and girls are two areas where some tough choices are needed. Delay school? Go part-time? And what about women? Should young riders avoid the drama and time of a serious relationship with the natural beauties that top-level cyclists often are able to attract? Phinney talked about having a girlfriend as he trained to qualify for the 2008 Olympics. "That was way too much work," he said. "I was madly in love with her and trying to race my bike at the same time." Phinney estimated he traveled a hundred thousand miles that year.

And college? "It's the same thing as having a serious girlfriend. You can't focus on one thing or another . . . I can always go back to school . . . There's always books."

Phinney felt comfortable here in Belgium surrounded by other young American cyclists. The Internet kept him connected to his home in Boulder. He referred to the young American riders who spent much of the racing season here as National Team Warriors. "I like to get in and get out, do the work I need to do," he said. "Cycling is a European sport. If you don't know how to race in Europe, then you're not going to be able to make it as a pro. It's really as simple as that."

Taylor Phinney does his own dishes in Izegem. Photo by Daniel Lee

Izegem was a quiet community. Its small central square offered only a few bars, and those seemed to be frequented by middle-aged folks out for an evening's beer. Locals here were curious about the Americans and their potential, like a basketball fan wondering if a college star could be a first-round NBA draft pick.

As I headed into the De Leest Community Center for the photo shoot, I chatted with a worker in a small office by the auditorium about the American team. In English, he peppered me with questions about the riders' ages, what races they had coming up. He wondered aloud whether the next Lance was among the riders getting their photos taken. As we talked, I carried with me a *Cycle Sport* magazine bearing the headline: TAYLOR PHINNEY: IS HE THE NEXT ARMSTRONG?

The American-Belgian cycling ties run deep in Izegem. American cycling fans passing through Izegem may do a double take when they see the sign for the Juwelier Bruyneel shop just off the square—the jewelry store is run by the family of Johan Bruyneel, the former Belgian pro cyclist who went on to a much higher-profile career as director of Lance Armstrong's teams during the Texan's seven Tour de France victories from 1999 to 2005.

Another former Belgian pro, Noel Dejonckheere, headed USA Cycling's National Development Team in Izegem from its start in 1999 before leaving in the beginning of the 2010 season for a director's position with the BMC Team. Even after his departure, the team remains based in the house attached to the Dejonckheere family Laundromat. Izegem grads are sprinkled across professional cycling's top teams: In 2010, David Zabriskie and Steven Cozza of Garmin-Transitions, Craig Lewis of HTC-Columbia, and Brent Bookwalter of BMC.

Tyler Farrar, six years older than Phinney, is another who pedaled this same path through Izegem on his way to becoming an emerging star of international cycling. In fact, Farrar is probably the most accomplished US sprinter since, well, Davis Phinney.

Like Phinney, Tyler stood out as a star at the USA Cycling house in Izegem. For both, the brick house on Kortrijksestraat has served as a sort of cultural bridge between the United States and Europe.

"There's a lot that goes into a pro cyclist. You have to be able to ride a bike fast. But you also have to be able to live and be happy. If you can't handle that then, you know, it doesn't really matter how fast you are. You're really going to struggle. That was a great thing about that program: It was a nice halfway step," Farrar said. "You come over; you get exposed to the racing over here. But you're living in a house full of other Americans. It's pretty easy. They take care of you. You're not worrying about all this other stuff. It gets your foot in the door. You kind of get familiar with the way it works. It makes it easier to make the next step as a professional living on your own over here."

And that's just what Farrar did. The native of Wenatchee, Washington, first came to Europe at age sixteen to race in the world championships in Portugal, and returned at seventeen to race in the Junior Tour of Flanders. He turned pro as a teenager in 2003, but even as he raced for the domestic-based Jelly Belly and Health Net–Maxxis squads he had it written into his contract to come to Europe for portions of the season and race with the US Development Team on the under-twenty-three circuit for Dejonckheere.

Farrar succeeded in both cycling worlds: In 2004 and 2005, he won stages of the Tour de l'Avenir, a closely watched race for developing riders. In 2005, he won the US Pro Criterium Championship. Dejonckheere said determined and talented riders like Farrar set a model that lifts an entire team. "They make their teammates 25 to 50 percent better." But he knew Farrar had outgrown his place in the US Development Team. "I tell him you are too good to race for me," Dejonckheere said. "The moment it's time to go, you go."

So, for the 2006 season, Farrar signed with the French-based Cofidis team. It was a dream attained, but also an adjustment as he left the American bubble of the US team house in Izegem to live in France near Monaco.

Until about May of that year, he needed race meetings translated from French to English. He sat as teammates laughed at jokes. "It made me grow up quick. I came to the team not speaking French, which was the first three or four months until I brought my French up to a good enough level. That was frustrating," Farrar said. He also lacked the results during his two-year stint with Cofidis.

This was a crucial point for Farrar. He thought about where he wanted to live. He had made friends in Belgium, yet Izegem was a small town. "I picked Ghent, not randomly, but I had only been here a few times," he said.

Ghent is a dense Flemish city of about 230,000 known for its canals, trolleys, and medieval buildings. Its famous Korenmarkt, or corn market, is a bustling center of churches, restaurants, and shops. Young people abound. "This is home for me at the moment," said Farrar, who now speaks French, Dutch, and a good bit of Spanish. For Farrar, 2009 was a breakout year that took off with a stage win in the early-season stage race Tirreno–Adriatico where he beat British super sprinter Mark Cavendish.

I met Farrar just a couple of days before the 2010 Tour of Flanders in Ghent. The Garmin-Transitions team bus, its side emblazoned with a huge photo of Farrar holding arms aloft in a victory salute, clearly marked the Hotel Europa on a side street as the team's base. Garmin mechanics tweaked and tuned the bikes that in a couple of days would compete in Belgium's most famous bike race.

Farrar crossed the small lobby on his way to getting his massage. The six-foot, 163-pound Farrar—then twenty-five years old—was lean but muscular; even the "bulky" sprinters of pro cycling are actually quite thin. His bright eyes and friendly smile reminded me a bit of Davis Phinney, the rider I had admired when I was a teenager. But Farrar's short blond hair sculpted up into a spiky faux Mohawk definitely gave him a hip look.

Farrar also stood out for his friendliness—confirming what I had heard and read, that he was one of the nicest guys in the peloton. We talked briefly as I told him about my idea to write a book about what it takes for Americans to race in Europe, and I told him I'd look forward to talking more with him at the Team Garmin press event.

Once the press event was about to begin, Farrar and three Garmin teammates—Canadian Svein Tuft, Dutchman Martijn Maaskant, and Scotsman David Millar—strolled in and sat at a table in front of a large montage of photos and signs promoting Garmin's GPS devices. All four riders wore their gray team-issue Garmin polo shirts. Millar stood out by wearing bulky UGG boots. This was one of those promotional appearances that is simply part of being a professional cyclist. Sponsors pay the bills. Garmin team director Matt White introduced the four riders, noting Millar's overall victory and Farrar's stage win in the recent Three Days of De Panne, a midweek race just before the Tour of Flanders.

Chris Baldwin, a London-based Reuters reporter, threw out a question about the importance of a rider's local knowledge in a race like the Tour of Flanders. His idea was to craft a story around the difficulty of these races, and of the disadvantage faced by riders who didn't grow up racing and training on these roads. Baldwin was taking pretty much the same angle for his article as I was taking for my book.

David Millar set the scene: "You have to know the roads. You have to experience racing on them. For such a long race there are very few actual key moments, and the lead-up on them can be on very technical small roads." Millar noted that many teams can build that local knowledge into their squads by signing Belgian riders. He added that Garmin has an advantage because Farrar lived locally in Ghent and knew the region.

The route for the Tour of Flanders is like a piece of music working itself into a frenzied crescendo: From the race's start in Bruges, the roads are relatively flat. But as the race approaches its finish in Ninove, the route becomes a series of short squiggly lines resembling a child's scribblings. Those tiny crooked lines are the narrow roads and the cobblestone climbs that decide each year's race, the lanes zigzagging across the same ridge of hills in southern Flanders.

In 2010, the first was the 450-meter Den Ast climb, later the more famous 2.5-kilometer Oude Kwaremont and 682-meter Koppenberg. The most drama of the race typically came on the second-to-last climb of the day: the Muur-Kapelmuur, a wicked cobblestone ladder that rises from the town of Geraardsbergen to its pleasant grassy summit where thousands of fans packed themselves around the chapel and crucifix. It came only around 14 kilometers from the finish of the 262-kilometer (more than 162-mile) race.

As I hiked up Muur-Kapelmuur a couple of days later, the steep hills and side streets of Geraardsbergen reminded me a bit of San Francisco.

Americans have rarely played leading roles in the Tour of Flanders. As of 2010, George Hincapie's third place in 2006 is the only podium finish for a US rider since the race began in 1913. Farrar was not playing up his chances for the 2010 race. I asked how he thinks his form is for Flanders. "Flanders isn't a sprinter's race, obviously. It's for more of an all-rounder. I'll go into it in good shape and hope for the best."

Then in another exchange during the press conference, Farrar displayed the awkwardness of a young American on a European stage. A Belgian asked Farrar whether people back in the States have heard of the Tour of Flanders.

"It's one of the few races that gets a bit more press. The two races everyone knows in the United States are the Tour [de France] and Paris–Roubaix," said Farrar, adding that cycling was growing in popularity.

"If you win tomorrow, will you be on TV or in the papers?" the Belgian questioner persisted.

"Ahhhh," Farrar said.

And then the Team Garmin's press officer interjected an emphatic, "Yes!"

The crowd of a few dozen laughed. But the truth was that a win in the Tour of Flanders would receive scant attention from the mainstream media. The sport in the United States was still defined largely by Lance Armstrong, the Tour de France, and—unfortunately—doping scandals.

A couple of days later, I stood atop the Muur-Kapelmuur, just yards from the chapel, and waited for the Tour of Flanders. I dug my shoes into the steep muddy roadside to keep myself from sliding down into the cobblestone road. Beside me a group of young drunk Belgians sucked down bottles of Jupiler beer and received their third or fourth warning from a stern but largely ignored female police officer to keep back from the racecourse.

First came the whirling sound of the helicopters, then the growl of the lead motorcycle up the steep hill. Fabian Cancellara's red-and-white Swiss champion's jersey flashed by just seconds after dropping breakaway compatriot Belgian Tom Boonen on the steepest part of the climb. Boonen, already defeated, pedaled by a few seconds behind, his face winced in pain. Americans Hincapie, Armstrong, and Farrar would soon pass by in what was left of the lead chase group.

The Europeans would rule the day: Cancellara grabbed a Swiss flag and waved it before crossing the finish line. Belgians Boonen, Philippe Gilbert, and Björn Leukemans took the next three spots, respectively.

At 2:35 down from the winner, the main pack of about thirty sprinted for the line. Farrar—who had crashed twice during the day—led the group in a long and painful sprint to finish in fifth, just ahead of fellow American Hincapie, the then-thirty-six-year-old veteran. Hincapie was nearing the end of his career—one defined by his role supporting Armstrong during the Texan's seven Tour wins. One of the young stars of American cycling, Farrar, was right next to him at the finish that day in Flanders.

Motivated Over Bicycling

To understand how American kids get into bike racing, you first should understand mentors like Mario Camacho. His hometown just outside Chicago seems better suited for blast furnaces than bicycles. The city sits amid northwest Indiana's foreboding industrial landscape of steel mills, refineries, and railroad tracks.

East Chicago, Indiana, had long been a place where the working class created middle-class lives from jobs at nearby mills and factories. That was the case with Camacho's family. His father, a Mexican immigrant, was a truck driver at one of the steel mills along the Lake Michigan shoreline.

For kids in the 1970s and '80s—when "I'll be home by dinner" was all that was needed before disappearing for hours—a bike was a young boy's escape to freedom. Camacho and his older brother rode to McDonald's. They rode across the gritty city streets into South Chicago. Young Camacho sometimes pedaled his Schwinn Varsity (a bike to be proud of at the time) eleven miles to his girlfriend's house in the hope of a kiss. When Camacho was about fifteen, East Chicago hosted a bike race as part of its festivities for Mexican Independence Day. He entered the race after some nudging from his brother. He wore blue jeans but felt like a star as he led the field of five for much of the race. Not even a kid in cycling shorts sprinting by him at the end could dull his elation.

The bike bug bit.

Camacho wasn't so much drawn to cycling for its power to produce heart-pounding suffering—as is the case for so many racers. Instead he reveled in teamwork and the feeling of satisfaction he gleaned from getting stronger and faster. One of his best memories on the bike was in college when a stronger rider dropped back from the pack during a training ride to pace Mario back up to the front group.

Mario and his wife, Nancy, eventually founded a bike club with some friends, naming it MOB Squad—for Motivated Over Bicycling. The club started as a simple collection of guys who liked bikes, but it soon developed into something more. Around 2001, Mario was at an Indianapolis bike race when he saw a middle-school-aged kid off the back of the pack in the citizens' race. But the kid never gave up.

After the race, Mario approached the kid, Guy East Jr., who became the first of a handful of teenagers to race for MOB Squad before advancing to the ranks of the elite. It was a case of cyclists inspiring cyclists. Soon after East got hooked on racing, Joe Kukolla walked down the hall at Indianapolis's Heritage Christian Academy and spotted schoolmate East's locker adorned with Lance Armstrong posters. The two started talking about their common interest in bike racing. Kukolla had also been talking cycling with teenage neighbor Adam Leibovitz.

Like East, Leibovitz would race for USA Cycling's National Development Team in Belgium. Leibovitz would become a national junior time trial champion in 2008 and elite pursuit champion in 2010. Another MOB Squad alum, Weston Luzadder, would win a 2008 national junior criterium championship. East would travel the world as an elite amateur and then a professional cyclist.

In America, kids grow up with a steady diet of baseball, basketball, football, and youth soccer. By kindergarten, they're in youth leagues with coaches and eager parents. Their parents played and understand these games. Competitive cycling, even in the age of Lance, remains outside the mainstream. Many kids get into bike racing because their parents are cyclists themselves. Others find the sport through chance encounters, or from mentors or friends. Most go years with little or no formal coaching, if they ever have any coaching at all. And being a skinny teenage bike racer who's shaving his legs before he needs to shave his face likely isn't going to attract the high school hotties. Cyclists aren't in the mainstream sports culture. They wear spandex, not jockstraps. Football players are jocks; cyclists aren't. Many bike racers are white and from the suburbs—kids in search of a different sports experience.

And becoming a cyclist offers an American teenager an identity and athleticism different from other kids. Camacho for years has taken his MOB Squad teenagers on rides over flat rural roads stretching out from his suburban Indianapolis home. "The wind is my friend; he makes me strong," he would tell them. He showed them how to draft in other riders' slipstreams. He gently corrected them for accelerating too fast in a paceline. He helped them form diagonal echelons to escape crosswinds howling across barren cornfields. Camacho called his approach "slow progression"—the joy of getting stronger in small increments, just as he did as a kid back in East Chicago.

I first met Camacho while we were students at Ball State meeting behind the campus bike shop for afternoon rides. Now I ride with him on MOB Squad's Sunday-afternoon training rides. Some teenagers join MOB Squad only to drift away within a season when they discover cycling is not their sport. But others stick with it, with the mothers or fathers of young riders sometimes taking part in the weekly rides. Camacho was young when he lost his own father, who died of a heart attack on July 4 while driving his truck at work. It was a day Camacho would never forget: About an hour after learning of his father's death, his brother's wife gave birth to a son.

Yet years later, Camacho found himself invited by another father—Guy East Sr.—into the inner circle of a son's ceremonial introduction to manhood.

In the fall of 2003, Guy Sr. invited a handful of men—close friends and mentors to Guy Jr.—to write letters to his son about lessons they had learned about God, life, and growing up. One man wrote about masturbation. Then Guy Sr. built a backyard bonfire and invited those men to gather with his son and talk about becoming a man.

Camacho, sitting by the fire, told a story he had heard before about frogs. He couldn't remember the source, but the tale perfectly reflected his own philosophy: Two frogs fell into a deep hole. They were desperately trying to hop their way out of their dire situation when other frogs gathered around the top of the hole. But the hole was deep and the frogs soon tired. The frogs up top sensed this hopelessness and started waving wildly and yelling, "Give up, it's no use!" One frog did give up, but the other seemed even more determined . . . jumping, jumping, jumping—finally hopping his way to safety. "Did you hear us yelling for you to quit? Why did you keep trying?" the frogs up top asked. "I couldn't hear you," the persistent frog replied. "I thought you were cheering me on." The moral, Camacho told East and the men around the fire, was that some in life would try to discourage you. Tune them out. Believe in yourself.

Guy Sr., who had an interest in cycling, had stoked his eldest son's interest in cycling from an early age. He bought a bike for young Guy and affixed an odometer to it. He was amazed to see his son, as an eight- or nine-year-old, putting twenty-five miles a day on the tiny bike—countless laps around the two-and-a-half-mile neighborhood circuit where he was permitted to ride. At age twelve, East rode behind his dad and family friend Dan Chapman. The two men soon heard a call from behind them. "Dad! Slow! Down!" Dad quickly gave a tough-love reply: "Deal with it; go faster."

Just a year later, thirteen-year-old Guy Jr. rode ahead of Dad and Chapman. Soon the father asked the son to, yes, slow down. "Deal with it, Dad," came the smug and satisfied teenager's reply.

Guy Sr., a former Purdue University tight end and long snapper, liked the show of attitude. Guy Jr. was a serious student. He'd go on to be an Eagle Scout. But Guy Sr. said his son was someone who didn't mind being lost in the crowd. And unlike his two younger football-playing brothers—who would both play college football—Guy Jr. didn't naturally excel at traditional sports. Chapman remembered trying unsuccessfully to coach East in youth basketball to simply catch and shoot without traveling. "He was nontraditional from the get-go," Guy Sr. said.

Cycling was a natural fit. The bonfire and a father–son road trip helped set East's drive to become a pro cyclist. In the fall of 2003, Guy Sr. loaded his son's bicycle into the family's green van and the two headed to the world professional cycling championship in Hamilton, Ontario.

Soon Guy Jr. was on his bike and scouting the course with the pros—an American teenager pedaling along with the Ukrainian team. Then he saw the US team. He hopped a barrier and joined a rolling collection of American cycling royalty: George Hincapie, Levi Leipheimer, Bobby Julich, and others. He tailed the US team for miles to its hotel. After being entertained by watching Floyd Landis pull wheelies in the parking lot, Guy Jr. realized he was far from his dad, moneyless, and exhausted. A merciful clerk at a Tim Hortons bakery gave him a doughnut for the ride back to his dad's green van.

After more than four hours of waiting by the van, Guy Sr. was relieved to finally see his exhausted-but-safe son return. In the weeks

A teenage Guy East on MOB Squad. Photo courtesy of Mario Camacho.

after that bonfire and road trip to the world championships, Guy Sr. saw big changes in his son. "It really defined and clarified his goals," the father said. East was a serious cyclist, his motivation sparked by his parents and a well-placed mentor, Camacho.

It's a classic American cycling story: a passion for bike racing ignited by another cyclist. Many millions of Americans enjoy riding their bikes, but only a tiny fraction of those ever race. In a nation of roughly 300 million, just 3,946 riders between the ages of ten and eighteen and 6,534 riders between nineteen and twenty-four held USA Cycling racing licenses in 2010. In contrast, more than 1.1 million American males played high school football and about 979,757 boys and girls played high school basketball across the nation in 2009–2010, according to the National Federation of State High School Associations.

With the right mix of talent and guidance from more experienced riders, the path to elite status can be a short one. With his slight five-foot-eleven, 137-pound build, it's easy to see why 2010 neo-pro Chris Butler found his love for cycling climbing the mountains of his native South Carolina. But those inclines aren't the only things he's been scaling: Butler has ascended from a Category 5, the lowest-level USA Cycling racer, as a Furman University student in 2007 to a pro with Team BMC in 2010. Yet unlike most new racers, Butler found a mentor in a Tour de France veteran, George Hincapie, after showing promise racing for the development team run by Hincapie's brother, Rich.

"He's a great climber, and if he continues to improve on his climbing as he gets older, he'll get even stronger," George Hincapie said. "If he learns how to position himself well in the peloton in these European races, he'll have come a long way."

Unlike many of America's most promising cyclists, Butler finished his college degree before jumping full-time into cycling. "It was pretty tough. Furman University is a small private school. Most people haven't heard of it, but it was a hard school. It was like four hours of homework a night. I actually was fortunate enough to get a scholarship . . . I actually ended up double majoring in economics and accounting. So, I mean freshman and sophomore years when I wasn't as serious, it was tough but doable. And then just last spring semester was pretty gnarly with all of the traveling, going to Italy mid-semester. So it got progressively tougher."

It's all cycling now, though. And he said long rides through the South Carolina countryside with Hincapie have prepared him for the life of a pro cyclist. "He's just the ultimate professional. He's so well mannered and polished. He knows how to handle himself, from training, to media, to everything. People pay so much money to see him . . . a charity dinner with him. I get to ride with him five hours a day by myself. I'm pretty lucky."

In the 1979 classic coming-of-age movie *Breaking Away,* fictional cycling-obsessed teenager Dave Stoller was a frightening lost soul to his father: a dreamy kid who shaved his legs and lived in a make-believe world of Italian cycling. That movie was made more than a generation ago—before Greg LeMond and Lance Armstrong sparked renewed interest in cycling. Even as bicycle racing remains a niche sport, there's now a community of parents who appreciate the sport. Some dads even shave their legs.

Ian Boswell, who rode for Team Bissell in domestic races and the National Development Team in Europe in 2010, would go on tandem rides with his father or watch his father race. He'd do kids' races in his native Bend, Oregon. By fourteen, he had won two national championships; a couple of years later he received an email from national team coach Benjamin Sharp. As a nineteen-year-old, he won the Best Young Rider competition at the Tour of Utah.

Daniel Holloway, who grew up in the San Francisco Bay area, started out with in-line skating. That wasn't fast enough, so he switched to short-track speed skating. The mix of speed and strategy of that sport suited Holloway's own intensity. Then Holloway's father enrolled his son in a bicycle track-racing program at the Hellyer Park Velodrome in nearby San Jose. "It was all about raw speed, just getting that adrenaline rush and suffering," Holloway said. "Track is just so raw and so close." He was still pursuing a career and track racing. But Holloway—a slightly stubby five-ten, 163 pounds—also had the build and temperament for road-race sprinting.

Holloway thanked his supportive parents for sacrificing their own time to support his cycling, spending weekends getting him to races. "I think he was a realistic dad," Holloway said. "He saw I wasn't a brain, wasn't getting A's, wasn't really motivated in school." (That's an interesting comment coming from Holloway. Throughout my months of reporting and writing this book, I found him to be among the most insightful young cyclists I met.) Holloway credited his dad with realizing that his son was a legitimate talent, and that pro cycling was a legitimate career path. By succeeding, Holloway said, he could justify the money his parents spent on him for new equipment or cycling gear.

Virginian Mark King, father of Benjamin King, joked that his son's journey to becoming a professional cyclist started at birth. Baby Benjamin was a red-faced maniac screaming with colic for the first six months of his existence—Mark said he was convinced that was when his son's aerobic capacity started to develop.

King, who by the age of twenty-one had raced for Kelly Benefit Strategies and Trek-Livestrong, is more introspective than brash. "He takes after his mom. He's a great student. He does really well in school," father Mark said. "He's just a good kid; never an ounce of trouble out of him."

Mark was a longtime cyclist himself who raced in his younger days for the Athletes in Action team. So cycling became a natural outlet for King. As a fourteen-year-old, he entered his first race: a criterium in Virginia Beach. During his warm-up, King was broadsided by a van and thrown ten feet from his bike. King was less banged up than his bike, so he took his father's bike, lowered the seat, and raced—finishing third from last in the under-eighteen category.

King—from North Garden, Virginia, near the university town of Charlottesville—excelled as a student and grew up with a group of close-knit friends from his church. He developed an interest in writing and earned top grades as a student at Virginia Tech. King talked excitedly of father–son elk hunting trips to New Mexico—of pushing each other on mountain bikes, and even of being a bit embarrassed to go shirtless back at the campground. "When you cycle all the time, your upper body just really disappears," King said.

Cycling may not have given King a buff chest, but it did provide him with an emotional and competitive outlet. He described himself as being a sensitive person, at times even a bit timid. Yet he also tells of an internal anger he can tap into when needed. As a sixteen-year-old, King was racing in a Category 1–2 (elite) criterium in the Tour of Shenandoah. He was riding midway back in the field but was stuck in the wind on the edge of the pack. King saw a gap between wheels and moved to position himself back into the energy-saving draft.

"Hey, watch it, junior!" screamed an older racer as he smacked King on the hip. King was livid—he rode aggressively through the rest of the race. "It's almost like your legs get emotional. It's almost like causing pain to the guy beside you is fun for you. It doesn't happen all the time," King said. "Sometimes you train and train and train, and just wait . . . and one race your 'angry' is there. You just have it."

Elite bike racing is about emotional decisions and risk taking. King spent two years at Virginia Tech, balancing his studies with bike racing. But he put his education on hold, a decision he made after barely being able to accept an invitation to train with Lance Armstrong because it conflicted with final exams. He needed to be totally available to bike racing. King has a panache for solo breakaways—a tactic that has earned him multiple national titles. Yet he said he was most proud of his decision to pursue cycling 100 percent.

Lawson Craddock of Houston also was lured into cycling by an involved father. Tom Craddock, Lawson's dad, was something of a bike pioneer himself—a Texas boy who moved to Crested Butte, Colorado, in the 1970s to be outdoors and to be part of the burgeoning mountain bike movement. Bike builders Joe Breeze and Gary Fisher were transforming twenty-six-inch single-speed clunkers into mountain bikes. Tom, who had competed in motocross, loved the thrill of being in the backcountry, of speeding around corners and past the many trees that lined the trails.

The responsibilities of adulthood eventually called Tom back to his native Texas: He got married, had kids, and started a roofing business. Tom had stopped racing but still enjoyed rides with his wife. Once the boys came, he pulled the kids behind in a Burley trailer near their Houston home. Then he rode with them on the tandem.

When Lawson was ten and brother Parker twelve, Tom entered the boys in a youth cycling program at the nearby Alkek Velodrome. "They both loved it, Lawson particularly. He had success from the very beginning," Tom remembered. Lawson, born in 1992, had grown up with the mix of sports so common for suburban Americans kids: He played youth soccer, a little basketball. He swam in a summer league and competed in junior high cross-country. Yet after that track camp—during which he won a new bike for his strong performance—he had found his sport.

By the time Lawson was fifteen, he was racing in USA Cycling Category 3 events—an intermediate level of racing contested by grown men. Tom rode many of the same races to look after his son, helping to keep him safe from crashes and well positioned in the pack. Lawson's father wasn't the only one watching him. After a string of top placings in the 2008 Joe Martin Stage Race in Arkansas, Craddock was upgraded to USA Cycling's Category 2—expert status.

Benjamin Sharp, who headed USA Cycling's junior program, also took notice. At the 2008 national championships, Lawson won the individual time trial in the junior category for riders aged fifteen and sixteen. What's more, his time of twenty-seven minutes, four seconds, was almost eight seconds faster than the time Adam Leibovitz—an Indianapolis kid who grew up racing with Guy East—posted to win the national championship for riders aged seventeen and eighteen. Sharp then watched Craddock lap the field to win the scratch race at the 2008 junior track national championships. Sharp was impressed by Craddock's ability to push himself: "One thing he can do is to really hurt a lot, which is something a lot of young riders aren't able to do."

In 2008, Craddock made his first trip to Europe with USA Cycling as part of a "fee-for-service program" where riders (or parents) pay their way to get international experience. He was part of USA Cycling's push to get promising riders European racing experience at young ages—while they were fifteen or sixteen, instead of seventeen or eighteen. In Belgium, Craddock got used to lining up with 150 other riders at junior races instead of the usual 15 or so back home. He got used to the more aggressive style; he learned the importance of riding at the front of the pack and elbowing his way up there if needed.

Lawson's full potential began to show at the 2009 UCI Junior Road World Championships in Moscow. The 25.8-kilometer (about sixteen miles) time trial course covered two laps of a circuit filled with ninety-degree turns, so bike-handling skills would be at a premium. By the time Craddock started, Australia's Luke Durbrige held the lead with a time of 32:52:23. Sharp had spotters on the course giving him times, so early in the race he knew Craddock was in contention for the win. Halfway through, he was down twenty seconds to Durbrige but gaining time. Each kilometer brought Craddock closer to a world championship. Sharp, riding behind Craddock in the team car, saw the Texas teenager riding a flawless race—hitting each corner smoothly at speed, keeping his heart and lungs on the edge of capacity. Craddock puked twice from his effort. The finish line neared.

Tom Craddock had made the trip to Moscow to see his son race. He had wished his son the best, said a prayer, and watched the time trial on a big screen set up for spectators. Craddock crossed the line 2.2 seconds slower than Durbrige's time. Tom paced not knowing where his son had placed until a Russian police officer told him Craddock had won the silver medal.

Lawson Craddock showed big potential in Moscow with a silver medal in the time trial at the junior world championship.
Photo courtesy of Lawson Craddock

In such close defeats in time trials, cyclists often dissect every bit of the race: A botched corner or a poor choice of wheels is blamed for costing precious seconds. Yet Dad, coach, and athlete were all satisfied. "Having observed every meter of that time trial, I know he rode the best race possible," Sharp said. Lawson was just as blunt: "I don't think I could have gone any faster."

It was a moment of affirmation and, for Craddock, joyous disbelief. Craddock, riding with Sharp in the team car after the time trial, remarked that he couldn't believe he had won a silver medal. It was a sharp contrast to the confidence shown by Taylor Phinney, an athlete raised by Olympians and surrounded by Tour de France stars from the time he was born. Phinney was brought up with international cycling and, according to Sharp, had an inner confidence his big victories would come. For Craddock, this was new. "It wasn't until after the event when he realized he had that potential," Sharp said.

Just as my friend Mario Camacho had said, cycling success is a "slow progression."

Izegem House Rules

One of the unspoken truths of group training rides is that different riders take varying amounts of time to get ready. Some riders simply dress, check their bikes, and are good to roll. Others find themselves searching like a style-conscious teenager for what clothes to wear. They fidget with their bikes. They raise or lower their seats by a millimeter. They recheck the shifting efficiency of their derailleurs. They have to go back inside after realizing they forgot to fill their water bottles. The less meticulous (or perhaps better-organized) riders find themselves waiting for the stragglers until the whole crew is ready.

This gradual process is one of cycling's rituals. It's time to talk. This scene played out at US National Development Team's house in Izegem on a chilly and blustery day in late March. Skinny junior racers looked almost burly bundled in tights, long-sleeved jerseys, and thermal vests. One by one, they gathered in the garage area tucked between the house and its attached Laundromat. Lawson Craddock chatted with his teenage teammates before the group headed out with coach Benjamin Sharp on an easy hour-and-a-half ride ahead of a hard weekend of racing. The topic was favorite foods. Craddock, from Houston, talked glowingly about the feast that is a "crawfish boil"—a Cajun tradition in which crawfish are boiled with ingredients such as sausage, potatoes, corn, and seasonings. Several of his US teammates, none from Cajun country, groaned in disgust at the idea of eating crawfish.

The topic quickly changed back to getting ready to ride.

"Do you have gloves?" Sharp asked Craddock as riding time grew nearer.

"No."

"Is this your first time here?" Sharp asked Craddock with a grin.

Craddock promptly retrieved his gloves. Finally the group was ready and rolled away from the house for their ride. The sounds of the cleats on the riders' shoes popping into pedals one by one could be heard above the gusting wind.

Each season since it opened in 1999, USA Cycling's Izegem house has brought together collections of riders from the many different regional climates and cultures that make up the United States. Remember, Copenhagen is closer geographically to Rome than New York is to Houston. The United States is one nation, but big and diverse. Junior- and under-twenty-three-level cyclists from states including Texas, Colorado, California, Wisconsin, and Pennsylvania were staying at the Izegem house during this stint in late March and early April.

Young riders such as Craddock can earn full expenses-paid trips to Izegem by impressing USA Cycling brass. Winning national championships is one way to get noticed. USA Cycling's Regional and National Development Camps, attended by more than three hundred young cyclists each year, are another way to shine. The camps include field tests to estimate a rider's power output, which in modern cycling has become a key measurement of potential. USA Cycling Vice President of Athletics Jim Miller said that a seventeen-year-old would stand out at camp if, over twenty minutes, he is able to produce roughly 4.5 to 4.7 watts per kilogram of body weight at lactic threshold. A promising junior racer such as Craddock is closer to pumping out 5.0 to 5.2 watts per kilogram. The power expectations build. A top under-twenty-three racer should put out roughly 5.5 to 5.7. A rider with the potential to land on the Tour de France podium could probably crank out 6.5 to 7 watts per kilogram.

What's more, according to Miller, the sport's top teams are looking to sign new riders at the relatively young age of twenty-one or twenty-two. It's a reality that can leave late bloomers behind. Riders who fail to land contracts with top teams may have few other options but to head back to the domestic circuit after they age out of the US National Team system at twenty-three. Miller, though, sees Americans as having an increasing advantage as more US sponsors and teams come into the sport. It's worth noting that four Tour de France teams in 2010—Garmin-Transitions, Team Radio Shack, BMC Racing Team and HTC-Columbia—were registered as American squads.

"There's no chance any of those teams are going to take a kid from Belarus over an American kid if they're at the same level," Miller said. "Zero chance."

Yet the reality remains that there are many riders for each available contract. So despite its sometimes fraternity-house atmosphere, USA Cycling's house in Izegem is a pressure-packed place for young Americans. Those who don't show progress in the eyes of the coaches typically are not asked to return.

Craddock, as an eighteen-year-old, spent around three months of the 2010 season racing in Europe, staying much of that time in Izegem. The young Texan showed plenty of promise. He had been a steady performer in international competitions and, in 2010, swept the criterium, road-race, and time-trial events at USA Cycling's Junior National Championships—something that had not happened in twenty-eight years. He was included in *Sports Illustrated*'s "Faces in the Crowd"—a brief feature that highlights athletes from around the nation—providing a rare bit of mainstream US media attention for a young cyclist.

Craddock doesn't worry about trying to stay in the same room during his different stints at the Izegem house. His focus is more on racing than accommodations. "I definitely learned how to live there," Craddock said. "It's not exactly home, but it's a good base."

The rooms are simple and sparsely furnished with bunk beds and perhaps a chair and small desk or table. Cycling clothes and laptops or other electronic devices are among the most common personal items strewn about the small bedrooms. The bedrooms may have small-paned windows. The bathrooms are European "water closets"—

There's nothing fancy about USA Cycling's house in Izegem.
Photo by Daniel Lee

tiny enclosed toilets. A paper sign taped to the wall shows a circle around and slash mark through a block drawing of a male figure with a dashed line representing urine coming from his midsection—the stream is missing the toilet and landing on the floor. The sign commands: REMEMBER: GOOD AIM, NO BABY WIPES & ALWAYS FLUSH!

Over the years, the Izegem house has developed its own subculture of rules and traditions, shaped mostly by Noel Dejonckheere and his wife, Els. Noel ran USA Cycling's Under-23 Development Program in Europe from its inception in 1999 through 2009 before joining the BMC Racing Team. While Dejonckheere guided the riders as they raced in Europe, Els kept order in the house. Her "Shit List"— written on the whiteboard in the common area—dictated domestic chores. She'd loudly reprimand those who dared to disobey.

"The Cave" is a windowless room reserved for staff or riders being quarantined while they're sick. These cyclists travel and race constantly so are often tired and worried about getting sick. The house gets messy, but coaches stress good hygiene because illness can spread fast with a dozen or more riders living in the same area and grabbing bread from the same loaves and cheese from the same bins.

The house, with all its quirks, can be a refuge from the tiresome routine of racing and traveling. International cycling requires almost constant transfers from one race to the next. Airports are full of delays, bad food, coughing people, and crying babies—all things that can sap energy and lead to illness.

Riders pass much of their free time in Izegem on the Internet checking social media sites or on Skype talking with friends and family back home. But laptops and other electronic gadgets are banned from the main downstairs common area of the house. Els deemed the devices antisocial because they prevented conversations around the dinner table.

"The Wall" is a favorite spot just down the street for an evening food run. It's a robotically operated bank of vending machines behind a glass wall that sells an assortment of items including snacks, tampons, and beer. The customer feeds the machine euros and makes a

The gang on a coffee break. Photo courtesy of Benjamin King

selection, and the robot fetches the item.

On days when riders are scheduled for easy training rides, groups of young Americans will pedal leisurely south from Izegem to Kortrijk for coffee. Clad in cycling tights, jerseys, and arm warmers, the riders chat as they sip strong espresso.

They also learn about the strange world of "Belogic," or Belgian Logic. These are some of the superstitions that pervade European bicycle racing and are sources of amusement for the young Americans: Don't shave your legs the day before a race because the process of the hairs growing back and poking through the skin wastes energy. Don't shower before a race because your legs will fill with water. Don't eat warm bread because it's still baking and expanding. Don't have plants in your room because they will take your oxygen.

The Americans don't feel bound to follow those guidelines. However, they sometimes break more logical rules as well. Stories of past pranks and misbehaviors at the house, perhaps embellished over time, are passed down like parables from older to younger riders. There's the time fireworks were set off in the house. Or the time one rider ran down the nearby street wearing nothing but an O. J. Simpson mask. Another tale is about a rider being caught pleasuring himself. Dejonckheere, when told about the incident, is said to have replied: "That's why we have stalled showers."

Another time, a couple of riders—one with some computer hacking skills—logged into a teammate's USA Cycling Web-based training profile and exchanged that rider's photo with one of a robust naked woman. Whenever a rider updated his profile, such as his weight, an email was automatically sent to Dejonckheere and top USA Cycling leaders. The hacking triggered just such an email—Dejonckheere reportedly yelled at the culprits with a bit of a smirk on his face. There's also the story of a rider spending the night in the Laundromat because the doors to the house lock automatically at 11 PM, the time of the house curfew.

In another busted-curfew caper, Guy East headed out into the

Izegem evening with a teammate in search of beer. First they tried "The Wall" before ending up scoring some brews at a tavern. Locals keep an eye out for misbehaving young cyclists. "Everybody knows why Americans are in this city," Daniel Holloway said. "So it's easy to go to the authorities—Els and Noel—to say, 'Your boys are having fun . . . too much fun.'"

East and his teammate returned from their beer run to find the house locked. They eventually pried open a window to get in and went to sleep. Early the next morning, Els walked through the house yelling, "Wake up, party boys! Wake up, party boys!"

The teammate was sent home because it was not his first offense. Dejonckheere told East that his race performance over the weekend would determine whether he had a future with the Izegem program. Inspired, East earned his keep by getting into multiple breakaways and finishing near the front of the field that day. It was the type of focused and feisty performance Noel longed to see from East.

Dejonckheere would evaluate each rider: Is he a climber? Is he a time trial specialist or a one-day classics rider? Then Dejonckheere probed for vulnerabilities. "What is your weak point? . . . If it's too weak, you're in trouble. You could be a really good climber, and if you can't ride on the flat you're in trouble." He'd then rate riders from 0 to 10 to help design their racing programs. If a rider was a 9 on the climbs and a 3 on the flat, Dejonckheere would line up a steady diet of flat races. Focus on the weakness. "That's the only way to make it in the long run," Dejonckheere said.

In professional racing, a rider's weaknesses are exposed quickly. In talking with riders and coaches, I repeatedly heard people refer to hard efforts in races as "burning matches." Each rider starts a race with a limited number of matches, and a climber who spends extra energy sprinting up the side of the pack on the flats because he is unable to hold his position near the front needlessly burns extra matches. A strong rider may start with ten matches, but wastes seven correcting his poor position in the pack. A savvier rider may start with just seven matches, but come to the finish line ready to ignite his remaining four matches in the final sprint.

Chris Butler is a boyish-looking climber who graduated from the under-twenty-three program to the professional ranks on such a program of races. "I'm still not good at kermises," he said. "I'm pretty weak in the crosswind . . . I'll have to work on that. But every time you do one you just get so much stronger."

In running the under-twenty-three program in Izegem, Dejonckheere built a reputation of being straight with riders about what he sees as their potential and being almost prophetic in his ability to read a race—to tell riders how they'll do before they hit the start line. He spent his career in European cycling as a professional rider. He then worked with the US 7-Eleven and Motorola teams before joining USA Cycling.

John Murphy, a sprinter from Georgia who spent the 2005 and 2006 seasons with the US team in Europe before turning pro, first arrived in Izegem just a few days before competing in his first race, Triptyque Ardennais, for the US Development Team. He remembered Noel telling him, "The race is probably too hard for you, but maybe you can just go there and see." Jet-lagged and overwhelmed, Murphy was dropped from the field.

"We'll keep trying," Dejonckheere told him.

Results came. Soon after his humbling first race he scored a top-twenty finish in the amateur Het Volk. Dejonckheere was impressed. As other results followed, Murphy noticed that his standing among his peers improved with his rankings on the result sheet. "You get back to the house and everyone treats you a little bit differently if you did well," Murphy said. "You could tell I had done well because everyone was all nice and happy. I was like, 'Oh you treat me differently now that I did well.'"

Murphy made his comments the day before he was set to race the TD Bank Philadelphia International Cycling Championship. He had taken what has become a distinctly American apprenticeship in cycling. He spent time with the US National Development Team in Izegem, turned pro, and raced with a smaller team on the US domestic circuit. Murphy won the 2009 US Professional Criterium Championship with Team Ouch. He then signed with the BMC Racing Team and is transitioning to compete in top European professional races.

Izegem is a place with an internal pecking order. Those who struggle fade. I once asked Daniel Holloway if he could think of some guys who had flamed out and were out of the sport. He barely paused before saying, "The guys that are racing are the guys who want to do it. The guys who decide not to do it, they are forgotten about relatively quickly."

Each rider must find his own way to cope. Benjamin King turns to his faith. During one trip to Izegem, he was rereading *The Problem of Pain* by C. S. Lewis. In the book, the Christian writer explores the reasons for human suffering. King wanted to keep the perspective provided by Christianity as he trained and raced with the others. "It's really easy to have friendships with the guys here because we have cycling in common," King said. "And when you have that in common and you get along so well, it's easy to become the group and just follow along with the group."

Yet King also has an irreverent and adventuresome side. Before one training ride in Izegem, he grabbed fellow US rider Andrew Barker's guitar and strummed and sang out Blake Shelton's "Ol' Red," a country song of how a man escaped from prison after he distracted Ol' Red—the warden's frisky tracking dog—with a pretty female Blue Tick hound.

"Ol' Red's itchin' to have a little fun," King sang.

A few days after his impromptu performance, King and Barker were out on their bikes to watch the Tour of Flanders—one of the races they aspired to compete in. The Flemish fans were partying and watching the race on TV in taverns as they waited for the riders to approach. King, on a damp chilly day, stripped off his jersey to reveal his bare pale-skinny-six-pack-abs cyclist's upper body. His winter Trek-Livestrong team cap and white-rimmed sunglasses completed his ridiculous look. He unveiled a large handwritten cardboard sign that read MAN-UP LANCE for Lance Armstrong. The locals loved the show of spunk: When King's jersey came off and the sign came out, they bought King tequila shots.

Ultimately Izegem is a serious place—a training ground for aspiring cyclists. But the USA Cycling house in Izegem remains one step on a ladder to the professional ranks that's still missing some rungs.

Washington State native Kiel Reijnen came to Belgium to race as an eighteen-year-old. First he raced for the Cycling Center, a separate facility near Bruges. Young riders from America and other nations apply—and typically pay—to live at the Cycling Center and race for its affiliated team. (The Cycling Center is more closely explored in chapter 8.) As a twenty-one-year-old, Reijnen then got a shot to come

Benjamin King shows his spirit at the Tour of Flanders.
Photo courtesy of Benjamin King

to Izegem and race for the US National Team.

Reijnen created his own path to reach his goal of becoming a professional cyclist. He enrolled in the University of Colorado at Boulder—long a hotbed of racing—to study engineering. He competed in collegiate races and raced for a strong under-twenty-three team. And while he appreciated the opportunities he had with the Cycling Center and with the US National Team in Europe, Reijnen said he also found the experience frustrating.

"You got over there. They gave you the starts at the races. They gave you the equipment. You got a ride to the race, and then they left you there and you figured it out. It was a steep learning curve. I learned plenty when I was there. But I think a lot of guys struggled. A lot of guys went over there and were kind of lost. They didn't have a knack for it," he said.

He saw resources and attention naturally flowing to the riders furthest along in their development—to those able to quickly score top results. "The guy who is finishing twentieth or thirtieth, he might have just as much potential as the other guy but nobody has the patience to really wait and find out."

Reijnen was not among those invited back to Izegem by USA Cycling to finish out his eligibility as an under-twenty-three rider. He also was frustrated with his experience at the Cycling Center. Yet he pressed on with cycling and signed in July 2008 with the US domestic-based Team Jelly Belly. Danny Van Haute, Jelly Belly's team director, said over the next two and a half seasons he saw a determined and maturing rider in Reijnen as he competed in major races such as the Tour of California and China's Tour of Hainan. By the 2010 season, as a twenty-four-year-old, Reijnen had blossomed into one of the better stage racers on the US domestic circuit.

Reijnen, unsatisfied with his first foray into European racing, took pride in his progress. He now has a specific goal: to get back to Europe, this time as a professional.

Bernard Moerman, who as director of the Cycling Center coached

Reijnen in Belgium, had this perspective on Reijnen's early frustrations with European racing: "Already then you could see his potential. I think he needed to grow up as a person first to really understand his own potential. Now he has grown into an adult and it is visible in his racing style and results."

It was, perhaps, a classic struggle between a coach and a strong-willed athlete. Yet cycling—unlike traditional American sports—adds the extra wrinkle of the athlete having to mature while also living and competing far away from home. Reijnen, the engineering student, has clearly thought about this in detail. He was frustrated by his first experiences racing in Europe, yet realized that the United States is still creating an infrastructure for building bicycle racers.

Reijnen knows that back in the 1980s when Americans Greg LeMond and Andy Hampsten were breaking into professional cycling, few other Americans made it because there was no system in place to help them. He credits organizations like USA Cycling and the Cycling Center for helping to show young Americans the path. But he sees many holes.

He contrasts cycling with baseball. From a young age, kids can learn from baseball camps, youth leagues, and traveling teams. High school offers promising players a chance to earn scholarships to play baseball at some of the top universities in the nation. Scouts pick out the best players for the professional ranks—starting with the minor leagues—where players are groomed for Major League Baseball. "Although we don't have the resources or budget to create a system like this overnight, I think it should be the goal," Reijnen said.

It's a laudable goal, no doubt. But it's one that is far from becoming a reality. Why? To understand the daunting challenges faced by US professional cycling, let's keep with Reijnen's baseball analogy. You will see that USA Cycling's program in Izegem is part of a puzzle that still has several key pieces missing.

The New York Yankees, and even perennial losers such as the Pittsburgh Pirates, are the pinnacle of baseball. The names and terminology of cycling's equivalent to the major leagues seem to be ever changing—from Division I to ProTour to ProTeams. But basically, it's the top rung of teams within the structure of the Union Cycliste Internationale, or UCI, the sport's Swiss-based international governing body. Just below that are Professional Continental Teams, which previously was considered Division II. These typically are the squads that compete in the big European races. The United States has been well represented at the top of the sport with teams such as Garmin, Radio Shack, and BMC.

Think of this as cycling's version of Major League Baseball.

However, most of the professional teams that compete on the US domestic circuit are UCI Continental Teams, formerly known as Division III—cycling's minor leagues.

These teams are sponsored by a variety of companies. There's Michigan-based vacuum-cleaner maker Bissell and Minnesota-based group insurance broker and consultant Kelly Benefit Strategies. California-based Jelly Belly, a maker of gourmet jelly beans, has been a stalwart sponsor on the US domestic circuit. These teams give riders such as Reijnen a start in pro cycling. Even after all these years of following cycling, I still marvel at the speed at which these pros can navigate corners in criterium races. And I love watching these small US teams try to compete against European-based teams in the bigger American road races.

But the UCI Continental Teams in the United States—by becoming the main players on the domestic racing circuit—have taken on a leading role that in some ways goes against their design. For any pro cycling team, the two goals are to gain exposure for sponsors and, of course, to win races. Yet Continental Teams are designed to do something else—develop young riders.

This intent is apparent in UCI rules: For 2011, a UCI men's Continental Team must have a minimum of eight and a maximum of sixteen road riders. If the team is registered with USA Cycling, 60 percent of the riders must have US citizenship. What's more, the majority of the team must have a racing age of less than twenty-eight years old.

Benjamin Sharp, USA Cycling's director of high performance endurance, understood the frustrations of riders such as Reijnen who think Izegem is a place where they are spit out of the system if they are slow to progress. But he added, "As a national team we really can't have anything more than a U23 program. That's where the onus goes on the Continental Teams to develop those riders . . . the U25 riders or the U27 riders. That's really the purpose of those teams. But in the US our system is so jacked, you know, some of our best teams are Continental Teams."

In Europe, he said, Continental Teams serve as feeder teams for the top ranks of cycling in a system similar to Triple-A baseball teams preparing players for major-league squads.

"In the US, cycling is like Triple A," Sharp added.

Yet for determined and talented riders, a spot on a US-based Continental Team can be a springboard to a contract with a big European team. Jelly Belly's Van Haute—who was a Team USA member for the boycotted 1980 Olympics in Moscow and the 1984 games in Los Angeles—said it bothered him at first to lose talented young riders to bigger teams. But he also pointed out that former Jelly Belly riders such as Tyler Farrar and Danny Pate have gone on to race in the Tour de France. "We develop riders," he said.

In recruiting new riders to Team Jelly Belly, Van Haute said he looks for sprinters and especially for young climbers. But he knows the best ones won't be with him for long.

Americans take many routes on the road to professional cycling careers. Reijnen struggled in Izegem, yet excelled at Jelly Belly. For Lawson Craddock—the teenage Texan fond of crawfish boils—the route has yet to fully unfold. Craddock, though, has tapped into some of the finest resources of US cycling's limited infrastructure. He raced for Hot Tubes, a highly successful junior development team. He was guided by David Wenger, a former professional and career cycling coach. He's become a top performer with the US National Team in Europe and, for 2011, signed with Lance Armstrong's Trek-Livestrong Development Team.

Sharp has seen Craddock grow in ability and confidence. He has seen the young standout perform cycling's grunt work—fetching water bottles from the team car for his teammates—in a stage race in which he won the time trial. It's all part of the process of becoming a leader. And it happens in the professional ranks as well. George Hincapie, one of America's most accomplished cyclists, spent a good bit of his career getting bottles and helping other stars.

Some junior cycling stars flame out after teenage successes. But Sharp doesn't worry about that with Craddock. "Lawson has an incredible work ethic and [a] rare ability to push himself super hard whether in training or in competition," Sharp said. "As long as he thrives off that sensation, he'll continue to be a successful bike rider no matter what level."

Craddock already has had to make hard choices in order to come to Izegem for cycling success. A serious student, he had long wanted to attend the University of Texas in Austin. He had the grades, was admitted, and planned to join his older brother, Parker, as a Longhorn. But Craddock instead ended up enrolling in the nearby Austin Community College in the fall of 2010 after, he said, the University of Texas told him he could not miss all the class time needed to accommodate his cycling schedule.

Remember Reijnen's wish that cycling was like baseball with top collegiate teams offering scholarships? Collegiate swimmers, football players, and baseball players may miss class, but it's all part of being an NCAA athlete. Craddock and other young cyclists can be in Europe racing with USA splashed across their jerseys. But they're simply absent from class, just like the kid who slept through the lecture because of a hangover.

"It's definitely disheartening," Craddock said. "But what are you going to do? It's life."

Despite those challenges, Sharp likes seeing young cyclists continue their education. "They need to get their collegiate career going so that when they do stop cycling or it doesn't work out, they're not starting from scratch," he said. Craddock is thinking about that. He wants to get a college education. He talks about eventually taking over his father's roofing business.

As far as his cycling education is concerned, Craddock has graduated from the junior to under-twenty-three US National Team at a time of great change. Dejonckheere, the clear ruler of the Izegem house, had departed for the BMC Racing Team. He knew the roads of Western Europe. He knew the races and how they would play out. He knew how to manage staff and evaluate riders. Yet even without Dejonckheere, Craddock and other young riders still head to Izegem to learn about their sport.

Craddock, at least for now, has sacrificed his goal of attending the University of Texas. But he still had a place in Izegem.

Cycling's Sad Side

One of my most memorable bike rides happened soon after Floyd Landis's now-disqualified 2006 Tour de France victory. My father and I rode for several hours through rural Lancaster County, Pennsylvania. We passed covered bridges, Amish families in buggies, and tidy farmyards with clothes hung neatly on lines. We simply enjoyed each other's company riding over country roads in a beautiful place. We made a special point of riding through the crossroads known as Farmersville to see the boyhood home of Landis, the Mennonite kid who had risen to become an international cycling star. He was a quirky character who had triumphed in the Tour de France a month earlier despite riding on a hip joint deteriorated from the results of a previous training crash. As with many US fans, I had been thrilled by Landis's Tour victory. And as with many, I was shocked by news of his failed drug test.

Landis was then in the early days of what would turn out to be almost four years of impassioned doping denials. In 2010, Landis would reverse course and confess to using performance-enhancing drugs. Yet in 2006, I wanted to believe him. His defense team accused the French Chatenay-Malabry lab of shoddy science in handling his test, which showed out-of-whack testosterone levels. The charges against him seemed dubious. He was adamant he was clean. I tended to trust him.

Before driving back to my parents' home in nearby Hershey after our ride, my dad and I bought locally baked pretzels, whoopie pies, and a shoofly pie—all delicacies of Pennsylvania Dutch Country. We then drove to Ephrata to the Green Mountain Cyclery, the bike shop where Landis got his start in the sport. I paid $20 for a yellow T-shirt with large letters reading HOMETOWN HERO above a photo of Landis on his time trial bike. Below were the words FLOYD LANDIS 2006 TOUR DE FRANCE CHAMPION. Landis's supporters had written messages of support on the large front window of the shop. I grabbed the marker in the shop and scrawled, STAY STRONG, FLOYD.

I was not one of those who donated money to the Floyd Fairness Fund for his legal defense, yet I had made an emotional investment in Landis that left me feeling betrayed and naive for being so thrilled by his exploits on the bike. Landis's story was not "Positively False," as his book boldly stated.

It was negatively true.

Bicycle racing has unseemly and sad sides that cannot be ignored. One is crashes—not simple spills that leave racers with road rash, but horrific accidents in competition and training that result in physical and mental trauma. Broken bones. Head injuries. Fatalities. The effect and treatment of crash injuries is explored later in this chapter. But the other piece of cycling's sad side is the plague of doping.

In reporting this book, I wanted to bring to life the aspects of professional bike racing that make it such a thrilling spectacle: lung-burning excursions, mind-testing strategy, and perseverance through the harsh conditions—a sport contested in beautiful outdoor settings. Yet the presence of doping must be confronted in any responsible examination of professional cycling and its culture. While I did not mention it to every rider I interviewed, the subject did come up.

Daniel Holloway talked openly about the issue. Our conversation came in June 2010, soon after the Landis doping confession. Landis, in a recent interview with ESPN.com, had said he slept better after finally telling his mom the truth. Holloway recognized lost integrity, lost authentic experiences, as the price of doping.

"There's not a lot to gain if you do it. You see all these guys, they get the results. They get more money," Holloway told me as we sat in a hotel bar in Philadelphia the day before the TD Bank International Cycling Classic. As usual, he wore his blue BIKEPURE.ORG anti-doping wristband. "But at the end of the day, you see Landis. He couldn't sleep at night. He couldn't live with himself. He couldn't even have a decent conversation with his mom, it sounded like. Once he told his mom everything that had happened, he felt better about himself. I couldn't imagine having to live with that on my shoulders. It's fake. My dad really instilled in me, do it the right way."

I asked him how dopers make him feel.

"Everybody in the peloton sacrifices blood, sweat, and tears—the clean guys more than the other guys because they're faking it. It's just frustrating when you try to do things the right way and there's that guy who doesn't care about anybody else. It only takes one guy to ruin a team, and it could only take one guy to ruin the sport . . . Right now cycling really has a dark cloud over it . . . Everybody has to look at what we're doing in anti-doping as positive. Everything is moving toward a positive step and showing people you can race clean and have top-notch performances."

Other riders voice similar frustrations. American Benjamin King said he has never seen doping. Yet the cheaters affect him: "You're stealing opportunities." And doping affects all riders in other ways that can be burdensome and undignified. They are grown men who must constantly update anti-doping officials as to their whereabouts. They must submit to random tests at odd times and places. And they must pee while being watched. According to the US Anti-Doping Agency, "The athlete will be asked to pull their shirt up to mid torso and pants down to mid-thigh" while providing a urine sample in the presence of a doping-control officer.

Jackson Stewart, a Californian with Team BMC, was once tested atop Georgia's Brasstown Bald climb in Georgia in the snow. He provided his urine sample in a portable toilet as the testing official held the door open to watch. Another time, Stewart was dehydrated and unable to urinate, so he sat in a public bathroom for three hours. "It's just awkward," Stewart said. "The guy was jammed in a stall with me." Yet Stewart said such invasions are worth it if it helps to conquer cycling's doping issue. He saw progress. "I am sure you can still

Daniel Holloway: "Everybody in the peloton sacrifices blood, sweat, and tears—the clean guys more than the other guys because they're faking it."
Photo by Daniel Lee

cheat; you always can. But now you'll get caught. In a career you'll get caught, it seems, whereas before you wouldn't."

Indeed, plenty of cyclists are caught and punished for doping violations. The USADA—the national anti-doping agency for the Olympic movement in the United States—has levied sanctions against cyclists sixty times (including multiple offenders) from 2001 through 2010. Only track and field, with eighty-four sanctions, had more violations than cycling. Dozens of Olympic and Paralympic sports—including archery, fencing, and table tennis—have had at least one athlete sanctioned over the past decade. Sanctions varied from lifetime bans for multiple offenses to public warnings.

Cycling's sanctions include high-profile cases such as Landis's two-year suspension in 2007 for "exogenous testosterone" and Tyler Hamilton's two-year suspension in 2005 for "blood doping" as well as his eight-year suspension in 2009 for an "anabolic agent." Some cyclists—and many other athletes—were punished after testing positive for THC, a primary intoxicant in marijuana.

Cycling can rightly say that it is among the most tested of sports in the United States. From 2001 through 2010, USADA performed more than 6,410 doping control tests on US and non-US cyclists, male and female, including some performed on behalf of other anti-doping or sports organizations. Only track and field, with more than 15,650 tests, and swimming, with about 7,700, had a greater number of total tests than cycling over that time.

USADA makes public a wealth of data on its website, usada.org, but does not tabulate or rank violations on a sport-by-sport basis. Such comparisons, in fact, are difficult given the vastly different numbers of athletes tested and tests performed in various sports. For example, USADA in 2010 performed 942 tests on cyclists, including multiple tests on many athletes. In that same year, it performed nine tests on table tennis players.

However, one way to get an idea of the prevalence of doping in cycling would be to compare a sport's sanctions as a percentage of its total tests from 2001 to 2010. According to my calculations, cycling—with 60 sanctions stemming in part from 6,419 total tests—had a sanction rate of about 0.93 percent. That was higher than swimming's rate of 0.17 and track and field's rate of 0.54. It also was higher than the 0.36 percent sanction rate of 266 sanctions out of 74,519 doping controls in all sports tested by USADA from 2001 to 2010. It should be noted that this, too, is an imperfect measurement of doping in sports, because some doping sanctions result from confessions or other evidence beyond failed tests.

These calculations, though, do seem to confirm the very real problem of doping in American bike racing.

Beyond all the tests and all the science, doping in professional cycling exists in a murky world of rumors and suspicion. Spotting a doper from the outside can be a bit like spotting other forms of dishonesty in society—who tells the world they are lying on their résumé, or siphoning money from the company account?

Dr. Dawn Richardson, an emergency medicine physician from New Hampshire, spent three years as a team physician for multiple US professional cycling teams. Yet as of 2010, she had stopped working directly in the sport because of what she saw as a culture of silence on the subject of performance enhancers that permeated cycling, even among those not participating in doping. "One of the problems in pro cycling is it's like touching the third rail. If you dare to say the word *doping,* everyone gets so upset with any association with their team," Richardson said.

Richardson said she herself never got a feel for how widespread doping was. And she got the sense the riders didn't really know, either. "There are lots of rumors. I certainly caught wind of an awful lot of rumor-mongering along the way," she said. Yet she made it a practice to talk with the riders she worked with about doping—bringing it up when she took their health histories during physical exams. "I tried to make it very clear that I was somebody you could come to confidentially," she said. "If you're a doctor you're like a priest: You can't violate the confidentiality." Richardson honored that doctor–patient relationship but did provide me with insight as to why cyclists go down the self-destructive road of doping.

As an emergency room physician, Richardson is used to sensitive topics and to lies from patients motivated by fear, denial, and embarrassment. She may push for a pregnancy test in a young woman who claims she is not sexually active but who has symptoms suggesting otherwise. She will tell patients injured after drinking and driving that she worried they have an alcohol problem and should consider treatment. "I just figured the only thing I could do as a team doctor, to be ethical, is just have honest conversations with the athletes about it and do what I could do to discourage them," Richardson said. "Or if guys who had maybe crossed the line and wanted to cross back, do what I could do to help them."

An academic study published in 2010 in the *Scandinavian Journal of Medicine & Science in Sports* highlights the degree to which many young elite cyclists struggle with the issue of doping. The study, by Swiss researchers, interviewed eight Swiss cyclists with an average age of just under twenty-three—six who raced in the under-twenty-three category and who hoped to turn pro, and two who already had turned pro. In the study, in which the participants were quoted anonymously, all the cyclists except one were tempted to dope. The study also found that at the elite amateur level, the influence of people outside cycling—family, girlfriends, fans, sponsors—and a "clean" atmosphere on cycling teams were among the influences not to dope. Conversely, the young Swiss cyclists said the most influential people at promoting banned substances were older cyclists who doped.

Richardson also noticed patterns related to doping. Some riders had a need for approval. They were willing to take ethical shortcuts to get the affirmation they were so desperately seeking. Some doped as a way to recover from an injury. Richardson said they rationalized their decisions: "If I take the shortcut and dope, then I'll be where I'm supposed to be if it hadn't been for that darn injury." She noticed that some of the riders who used performance enhancers had substance-abuse problems, such as alcoholism, before they were professional racers. Once a rider has started down the road of doping, it can be difficult to turn back, Richardson said. A friend of hers once compared it to a rehabilitated bulimic heading back to the supermodel runway—she is right back in that temptation-filled environment. "Some people have handled it successfully," Richardson added.

During the time Richardson was writing the "Ask the Doctor" cycling medicine column for *VeloNews,* she started reaching out to riders who had positive doping tests.

"How are you doing?" she'd ask. "Any depression?"

She said the response often comes back, "How'd you know?"

Richardson would tell them they were not alone. She would suggest counseling or treatment. She would tell them it was going to take some time for them to come to terms with what they had done. "I think they had no idea what the social and psychological consequences of a positive [doping test] were going to be. They had no idea how badly a positive would damage them, damage their plans, what they thought of themselves."

Richardson's comments about the emotional burdens carried by some sanctioned dopers made me think back to an interview I had with three-time Olympic cyclist John Howard, a pioneer in American road racing during the 1970s, before the country had an organized professional circuit. I had asked him if he saw many drugs in his day. Howard said: "We were never tempted because it was never offered to us. We didn't have the soigneurs. We didn't have the team doctors. We were just green amateurs racing against professionals. We were good. We had our day. I look at it today, and I'm just so glad we were never in a position to be corrupted . . . I watched some of these guys climbing in the world championships in Montreal—these are guys I've ridden stage races with, the Tour of Britain, the Tour of Ireland. I wondered, how are they climbing Mont Royal in their big chainring? I can't do that. I can't get that kind of power. Maybe the justification for that is I'm still enjoying my bike and some of them are gone. So I think the payback, if there is one, was longevity. To me, that's what cycling was all about, always has been. It's the fresh air and the blue sky and the fact I'm going to be doing this for the rest of my life."

Doping, of course, is not the only physical and emotional hazard of professional cycling. While doping in the end is a personal choice, crashing is not: Every rider eventually hits the deck. During my visit with the US National Team in Belgium, the topic of injuries and crashes did come up sporadically. The riders talked about crashes in a matter-of-fact way. Holloway remarked that crashing is part of the sport. Another rider, upon hearing about a crash in a women's race, said, "That's why pretty girls shouldn't race bikes." Racers also talk about the harsh elements of racing—cold rain, treacherous courses—as opportunities for more determined riders to defeat lesser foes.

Dr. Eric Heiden saw such determination in the 1980s when he

was a professional cyclist, and continues to do so now that he works with top racers as an orthopedic surgeon. Heiden is most famous for winning five gold medals in speed skating at the 1980 Winter Olympics in Lake Placid, but he also made cycling history as a member of the 1986 7-Eleven squad, the first American-based cycling team to compete in the Tour de France. Yet he was forced from the race after crashing on a descent and sustaining a concussion.

I asked Heiden if the crash affected him or made him more aware of the risks. "At that time, no. I was so focused on cycling," he said, adding that it's just part of the mentality of elite cyclists. "They fall off their bike and their first inclination is to find their bike and get back on it, because the race is going down the road and if they don't get back on their bike it's all over." Cycling, unlike many other sports, has no injury timeouts. It's only after riders remount and are pedaling again that they take an assessment of what hurts, what's working, and what's not. "Sometimes that's to their detriment, you know. Gosh, you have a head injury and the last thing you want to do is get back on your bike," he said.

Those tumbles, though, eventually took a toll on Heiden during his cycling career. "I sort of lost that fearlessness when it came to the sprints just because I got tired of getting injured and having to recover from that injury," he said. "It was time to move on and do something else because you cannot have something like that sitting around in your subconscious or consciousness. It will affect you." Such fears can't be dominant in a racer's mind in the midst of a chaotic field sprint or high-speed descent.

And so Heiden, after earning a medical degree from Stanford University, started his third career—as an orthopedic surgeon specializing in sports medicine. He's been on the medical staff of the NBA's Sacramento Kings and team physician for the US Speedskating Team during the 2002 Salt Lake City Winter Olympics. His experience with cyclists has included working with members of the US National Team and the professional BMC Racing Team. What he found was that the same grit that motivates injured riders to remount their bikes also makes them motivated but tricky patients to treat.

With the general population, it's easy for doctors to prescribe a little rest. But with elite athletes, inactivity is equated with falling behind. There's always a race to prepare for, the next contract to secure. Heiden sees this trying to deal with riders with broken bones or overuse injuries such as anterior knee pain. Time off the bike often is not an acceptable therapy. Richardson tells similar stories: "They always seem to want to speed up the timetable of their recovery. You break your wrist; you get your cast off two weeks before it's supposed to come off. They just feel the need to do that. It's not necessarily in their long-term medical interest."

Increasingly, medical researchers are raising concerns that professional cyclists don't just have thin bodies, but also tend to have thin bones. Low bone-mineral density can put cyclists at high risk for fractures in a sport that already has a high risk for fractures. Cycling, unlike running, is a non-weight-bearing activity. And that can deprive riders of the daily impacts and stresses on the skeleton that help to maintain strong bones. The study "Bone Status in Professional Cyclists," published in 2010 in the *International Journal of Sports Medicine,* compared the bone-mineral density differences between thirty professional road cyclists and thirty healthy males with the same average age, around twenty-nine. After adjusting for differences in age, height, lean and fat body mass, and calcium intake, the researchers found that the cyclists had lower bone-mineral density just about every place below the skull—arms, legs, spine, pelvis, and neck of the femur. Heiden said he has seen cyclists break a wrist or other bone in a seemingly incidental fall.

In sports such as basketball and soccer, running is a natural part of the game. Football players hit the weight room as hard as they hit opponents. Coaches punish players by making them run. Many cyclists see little benefit to such bone-strengthening activities. Heiden said it does not seem that muscle strength gained in the gym is immediately transferrable to cycling. Some riders may cross-country ski or snowshoe in winter. That's good cross-training, but those activities also provide little impact on bones. Many cyclists spend the off season in the basement on turbo trainers.

"At the elite level, it's very hard to find more time to train, so you have to be very efficient in your training. The most efficient way to train is being as sport-specific as you can," Heiden said. "It's hard to get those guys off a bike."

Taylor Phinney—a beefy guy by cycling standards—raised the issue in a joking manner when I talked with him about his potential of improving his climbing to become a contender in mountainous stage races. "The endurance factor comes in later when I'm in my late twenties and I'm lighter and have zero bone density because I've been riding a bike for too long."

I asked him if he worried about that.

Phinney replied that a scan found he had above-average bone density. He credited a youth spent playing soccer, running up and down mountains, and—as he put it—jumping off things. "I have big strong bones."

Yet each cycling season brings a new batch of broken bones and assorted other injuries. American veteran Christian Vande Velde has been a one-man orthopedics project: In May 2009 at the Giro d'Italia, he crashed and broke five vertebrae, his pelvis, and ribs. He recovered in time to finish eighth at the Tour de France in July. But 2010 brought more traumas: a broken clavicle in the Giro, three broken ribs in the Tour de Suisse, and two broken ribs in the Tour de France.

Bicycle road racing, because it is not confined to a stadium or arena, holds an ever changing array of hazards for its participants. Riders can be injured by dogs and cars veering onto the course at just the wrong time. Curbs, guardrails, road signs—designed to improve traffic safety—are potential bone breakers within cycling's field of play. Riders negotiate hundreds of these dangers every race.

In 2007, then-twenty-three-year-old Brent Bookwalter—now one of US cycling's most accomplished young pros—was used to the rolling chaos that is high-level European racing when he was with the US National Development Team at the Triptyque des Monts et Châteaux in Belgium.

It was Easter Sunday, and the international pack of young elite riders roared into town onto cobblestone streets for the final circuits where that day's stage would finish. Bookwalter knew the drill. When racing on cobbles, look for any smooth shortcut possible. Ride in the gutter if it's smoother. One useful skill in Belgian racing is an old BMX trick known as the bunny hop—using your hands and feet to lift a bike—at race speed—up and over obstacles. In the final kilometers, riders were doing just that. They jumped from the cobbles onto the sidewalk to advance their position in the pack, and then hopped down from the curb again.

Bookwalter started his own bunny hop when something happened: He tangled with another rider. He lost control and, at full speed, hit a light pole with his lower left leg. He looked to see three or four inches of his tibia sticking out through the skin. People swarmed around him to help. For Bookwalter, the pain and the sight of his own bone were indescribable. He tried to move his leg, only to see his shin flop. He asked Noel Dejonckheere, then director of the US team, to hold his leg. "The first EMT responders on the scene, they kept telling me they needed to clean it . . . That was just absurd to me. That was the last thing I wanted to hear. I was like, 'Get me to the hospital! Get me off the street!'" Bookwalter said. "Fortunately, we were really close to the hospital. It was a short but intensely painful ride down the same cobbled street we had just had just raced down to the hospital."

Since it was Easter, an orthopedic surgeon had to be called in from home to operate on Bookwalter's shattered shin. He was numbed from the waist down and a sheet was put up to block his view of the surgery. He heard drilling and pounding. He heard conversations, but this was the French-speaking part of Belgium so he couldn't understand what was being said about him or his condition.

That instantaneous crash would sideline Bookwalter for eleven months. He went from being a recent graduate from Lees-McRae College in North Carolina on the verge of a pro cycling career to moving back in with his parents to face months of rehabilitation. Setbacks happened along the way. During one doctor's visit, his orthopedic surgeon took a long look at his X-ray and said, "Hmmm." The surgeon wasn't so crazy about the hardware used to fix Bookwalter's leg and worried whether the bone would grow back properly. After weeks of waiting—and after the doctor bent Bookwalter's shinbone like a hunting bow—a second surgery was performed in July to redo the leg. He underwent a rigorous course of antibiotics—by IV for six weeks and orally for six months—after he showed signs of infection.

During one appointment, a doctor told Bookwalter, "You're just going to have to learn to be a couch potato." Frustrations boiled over. "That just wasn't acceptable to me," Bookwalter remembered thinking. "I was like, no. I don't care if I'm sitting on the floor with some dumbbells like punching in the air . . . There's got to be something I can do. The average patient that the orthopedic surgeon sees isn't addicted and obsessed with physical activity like we are."

Heiden, through his role with USA Cycling, would look at Bookwalter's X-rays and encourage him. Gradually, Bookwalter returned to a more active life. He lost a crutch while kayaking. He went to the beach. By August, he was spinning on an indoor cycling trainer—using his healthy right leg to power the pedals. Skin-tight cycling shorts were baggy on his atrophied left leg. For his first ride outside, he took his mountain bike, lowered the seat, and tooled around a grass field. Bookwalter was the least fit he had ever been, but he was back. And slowly, the form that had made him an elite racer returned. At team BMC's training camp in 2008, he used compact cranks to allow for a smaller (easier) chain ring because his legs lacked the strength to turn standard gearing. Late that season, a full year after he started riding again, he was feeling powerful again. He could hurt himself again—the good kind of cardiovascular hurt cyclists long for—during a race.

Bookwalter now has completed the Giro d'Italia and the Tour de France. He's become a seasoned pro. The crash, he said, made him realize how much he loved cycling, how much it was part of his life. "It sort of reignited the fire." But effects from the trauma linger. His leg can still bother him in the cold or after travel. Bookwalter also has what he calls "hard-object anxiety." Yet he has also accepted that his job requires him to sail through European towns on a bicycle, by countless light poles and road markers.

"That's all part of it. We do that every kilometer of every day."

8

Kermis Culture

I downed my third—perhaps fourth—cup of strong coffee at the Hotel 't Oud Wethuys in Oostkamp, a charming if sleepy Flemish town just south of Bruges. Morning chimes from the neighboring cathedral filled the air outside this chilly morning in early April. Yet the sounds of church bells carrying into the breakfast room were but a pleasant distraction from my intense conversation with Bernard Moerman, who for almost two decades had operated what has become a Belgian base camp for hundreds of young Americans hoping to climb the ranks of European cycling.

He knows it's a tough ascent for even the hardiest Americans. "You can be the champion of a state and not make it two laps into a kermis over here. I want to detect more whether you have the character to bike through all this, to learn, to be coachable," said Moerman, his deep Flemish accent carrying the urgent tone of a professor reaching a key point in his lecture.

The Cycling Center, directed by Moerman, has become a study-abroad program for American riders, especially for those who are not part of the US National Development Team in nearby Izegem. It's a place to live, eat, and learn Belgian cycling. Residents at the Cycling Center become members of the Moerman-directed Fuji Test Team. The squad's roster of more than twenty spanned the globe with riders from Belgium, Finland, Malta, Canada, Australia, and across the United States. Most are in their early twenties. And many riders are paying their own way to be part of the center, typically around 1,000 euros (almost $1,400) a month for room, board, and—of course—racing.

Fuji Test Team members get a steady diet of local Belgian kermises, the locally organized and famously tough circuit races held almost daily throughout Flanders. Riders enter kermises, typically 120 kilometers long, as individuals, not as part of a team. Cycling Center riders also get a chance to test themselves in "interclubs" —UCI-sanctioned races—which typically are 150 to 180 kilometers in length. In those races, riders compete as part of the Fuji Test Team.

Some Cycling Center alums, such as American Jeff Louder, have gone on to join the pro ranks. Yet for others, it can be an expensive and frustrating series of setbacks on the bike. In 2010, the Fuji Test Team was a mix of experienced riders like Peter Horn—a Colorado native who had his costs covered by Moerman—and Euro-racing rookies such as Addison Bain of Minnesota and Nathaniel Thompson of Maryland. Horn, born in 1985, edged ever closer to a pro contract with a European-based team. Thompson, born in 1985, and Bain, born in 1989, focused more on simply finishing races. By the season's end, all three planned on returning to Europe for more racing. But they also were making plans for futures beyond cycling.

A former professional soccer player in the Belgian league, Moerman stumbled into cycling in the early 1990s after an acquaintance asked him if he could host a US rider in Belgium. Moerman previously had little detailed knowledge of bike racing, but he was drawn to the toughness of the sport. He was used to the world of pampered professional soccer players and was shocked to see elite bike racers, after racing in harsh conditions, given only a small towel to clean themselves off. He said he wanted to provide Americans coming over to race with a comfortable place to stay: a bed, a bath, and some guidance.

Moerman has tremendous respect for the young Americans who come to Belgium to race. They leave girlfriends and generally comfortable lives to, in most cases, be humiliated when they are blown off the back of the pack in the opening kilometers of their first races. They are, at least for a time, failures in the very sport from which they draw their motivation and self-identity. "Hey, you're not the only one," he tells them. George Hincapie and Levi Leipheimer traveled the same road.

According to the gospel of Moerman, Americans first need to understand the hard-knocks culture of Belgian racing. "Here it's business and business only. In America, it's a big part fun. It's a social happening in America." A typical American criterium is a daylong activity: races for women, for racers forty and older, fifty and older, separate events for USA Cycling's five skill categories. "Here, there is only one race: yours. You get there, do your stuff, and go home. For a lot of riders, that mentality just blows them out of the water."

Most American riders are decent athletes, he said, but not yet bike racers. That distinction comes when a rider is able to successfully battle for position in a pack of two hundred, where fifty are capable of winning. Moerman pointed out that from what he's seen of US racing, a big field may have more than a hundred riders, but only ten or so realistically stand a chance of winning. The average speeds of races also can be deceiving. In America, a race may average forty-four kilometers per hour (twenty-seven mph) but the slower portions of the race drop to thirty kph and the faster parts reach fifty-five kph. In Belgium, a race may average that same forty-four kph but have a range in speed from an agonizingly slow ten kph in a corner onto a narrow lane to a blazing sixty-five kph down a smoothly paved road. It's a competitive elasticity that can sap the legs of even the strongest of riders if they aren't cagey enough to know how to position themselves in the pack. Some of the young Americans at the Cycling Center were preparing to race a kermis that afternoon.

Moerman excused himself from my breakfast table and headed off to his next appointment. I walked out of the Hotel 't Oud Wethuys, which also happens to be run by Moerman and his wife, and made the short walk up Brugsestraat to the Cycling Center. The sturdy light brick building sat close to the road next to a photography studio and hair salon. The brick driveway ran underneath the building to a backyard filled with Fuji team vehicles. A few chickens strutted and clucked in a small pen behind a nearby house. I walked through the back door and into the center's main living area.

The Cycling Center, with simple block walls, is not fancy. It seems similar to a newer small dorm: clean and comfortable but clearly inhabited by young males. The main room has a long table for gatherings and a small kitchen. Titles on the bookshelf include *Speaking Dutch with Ease* as well as *Breaking the Chain: Drugs in Cycling—The True Story,* which is former soigneur Willy Voet's account of the 1998 Festina doping scandal. Other books on display, such as *On Bended Knee: The Press and the Reagan Presidency,* seemingly are out of place and rarely touched. However, many riders are students or curious people who may look for all kinds of reading—literature, history, politics, philosophy—to escape from the routine of racing and living in Belgium.

I heard voices and wandered upstairs to a small living area with a kitchenette. Addison Bain was finishing his own breakfast of chicken and mac and cheese. Nathaniel Thompson sat nearby. Both were new arrivals in the Cycling Center.

Thompson—who has a thin-but-sturdy build and a passing resemblance to actor Matt Damon—got into bike racing when he was a sophomore at Washington College in Chestertown, Maryland. He was drawn to cycling in part by his older brother, who had raced. Thompson, who raced dinghy boats on the Chesapeake Bay, started out just wanting to ride. But soon he got into the competition and strategy of road racing. He took time off school to race in Colorado. He advanced through USA Cycling's ranks to become a Category 1 racer. He was attracted to the complexity and culture of bike racing—that a tactically superior rider can defeat a stronger foe. He worked as a bike mechanic to help pay for his season-long stay at the Cycling Center, calling it an opportunity he could not pass up.

Yet he was already twenty-four—an advanced age for a US rider to first venture to Europe. And Thompson was off to a rough start. He dropped out of his first race after the metal plate holding the handlebars to his stem came loose. His second race brought a much bigger setback: In a rainy interclub in Trognée, Belgium, he crashed into a rider who had fallen in front of him. Not seriously hurt, he chased back through the race caravan and back to the pack. As the pack approached a right-hand turn, riders suddenly slowed to make it through the turn—the dreaded accordion effect. Thompson squeezed his brakes hard. His handlebars hooked onto a nearby rider's bars, hurling Thompson chin-first to the ground.

A broken jaw . . . and loosened (but thankfully unbroken) teeth.

"I'm lucky I didn't have to get my jaw wired shut. The hardest part was not being able to chew anything," Thompson said. He used a blender for every meal for three weeks. He hadn't raced over that time. "I can't wait to get back."

Thompson wouldn't be racing this day. But Addison Bain would. The then-twenty-year-old Bain had left his studies at Lindenwood University in Missouri to come to the Cycling Center in March. "I wanted to ride my bike," he said. As with Thompson, Bain—a Category 2 racer—said the goal is to go pro. Bain had a tattoo on his arm that reads, LET THEM HATE SO AS LONG AS THEY FEAR. Yet Bain, who had a round boyish face and mussed morning hair as he finished breakfast, also clearly had struggled getting used to living in another culture. "It's just a totally different mental game over here," Bain said. "You don't get a rest." I asked him about approaching Belgian girls— after all, these are young guys spending months away from home. "I don't know," Bain said. "They're different. They're really shy."

Other riders offered a different perspective. Peter Horn said Belgian women are straightforward and sometimes downright forward if they see something or someone they want. According to Horn, the Cycling Center veteran, in the United States it's a real game to get to know women and ask them out—it's much simpler in Belgium.

Bain's Canadian teammate, Jannes Wessels, jumped in: "All we do is ride our bikes, sit around and eat and watch TV. There are really not a lot of social places that our lifestyle includes." Wessels then conceded he had a girlfriend back home.

Facebook, Skype, and other Internet pursuits fill time. The Cycling Center riders made regular trips on foot or "beater" bikes to buy the chicken and pasta that made up much of their diet. Belgian TV—unfamiliar game shows and American films dubbed into Dutch—held limited appeal. As I left the kitchenette and TV room, I noticed a DVD of the Audrey Hepburn musical *My Fair Lady* sitting out in plain view. "Whose is this?" I asked, pointing to the DVD. No one claimed to have watched it or knew where it came from.

I headed outside to the garage area and found Peter Horn of Colorado, one of the Cycling Center/Fuji Test Team's most promising riders. This was Horn's sixth year with Moerman at the Cycling Center. And because he was a proven talent, Moerman was covering Horn's costs to be part of the Fuji team. Horn was preparing to race that afternoon in a nearby kermis. Sometimes racers ride to the competitions for extra miles before and after the kermis. But Horn had rented a car for this special occasion—his girlfriend, Maya Barolo-Rizvi, was visiting from the United States. The three of us, along with Horn's Fuji racing bike, crammed into the compact car for the roughly twenty-minute drive to the race.

For this early-season kermis on April 5, the then-twenty-four-year-old Horn did what just about every cyclist does when arriving for a race: He found race registration. It's typically in a bar or café, and this kermis was no different. Outside the Café den Drieweg in the Flemish village of Zwevezele, a man grilled sausage as locals sat drinking coffees and sizing up riders warming up on the course. Bain and Wessels, already registered, tooled around on their bikes warming up on a cloudy but dry afternoon. Inside this smoky bar tucked into the Flemish countryside, Horn walked up to the table staffed by gray-haired race officials and plunked down his entry fee of 3 euros (about $4).

"Primes?" Horn asked.

"Every second lap," replied one official. "Primes," or lap prizes, were standard in kermises. Horn was the 106th and final entrant for this twenty-lap, roughly sixty-mile kermis. Horn, a 2008 graduate of Vassar College in New York, had put law school plans on hold as he

Race headquarters for a spring kermis. Photo by Daniel Lee

pursued his pro cycling career.

Horn grabbed his race number from the stack but no safety pins. Remember, in Belgium, you bring your own pins to races. An afternoon of crazy kermis racing was about to begin. Belgium's tight roads and crossroads cause packs to split up early, so riding at the front is vital. Kermises also are famous for deals cut among the top riders—but to be part of a deal, you have to be at the front.

Young Americans will tell of how the aggression starts before the race. US riders new to the scene pull up to the start line early, thinking they've secured a spot at the front. Then just minutes before the start, Belgians pull up in front of them and back their way into the front of the field, or they move a barrier to cut in. Others may lean against a nearby building, clipped into their pedals, ready to pounce to the head of the race. Once the race is going, Belgians jump sidewalks and curbs to gain position. And *"Godverdomme!"* (a multipurpose swear word meaning "Goddamnit") is likely to be one of the first Dutch words an American racer learns.

Horn was used to this stuff. He had competed in more than a

hundred Belgian races, with some top placings. So in this race, he worked his way into a breakaway of seven within the first few laps.

While the Belgian racers like to yell, the mostly older fans who lined this course take a quiet approach. Elderly men holding beers watched and discussed the race as the strung-out pack whirled by the start–finish area before making a sharp right-hand turn from a wide two-lane road onto a narrow farm lane.

Barolo-Rizvi, Horn's girlfriend, yelled, "Go, Peter!" as the break-

Peter Horn, second, makes the breakaway. Photo by Daniel Lee

away passed. With her long black hair and stylish leather boots, she stood out among the crowd of mostly retirement-aged Belgians. An elderly Belgian fan heard her and asked, "With you?" Barolo-Rizvi nodded. The man smiled and nodded in return, impressed by the American in the breakaway.

Near the finish line, Belgian bike bookies posted the names of riders with odds on whiteboards. Barolo-Rizvi had placed a 15-euro just-for-fun bet on Horn before the start of the race—a bet that would have landed her 175 euros should he win, or about 12 to 1 odds. Once Horn was in the breakaway, though, Horn's odds had improved to either 5 to 1 or 4 to 1, depending on the bookie.

He looked strong as he clung to the wheel in front of him in the

Odds posted for riders and the sausage cart are two constants at kermis races. Photo by Daniel Lee

crosswind on the small Belgian lanes. He grabbed a bottle along the backside of the course from Canadian teammate Wessels, who was caught behind a crash early in the race, his ankle bloodied from stepping through someone's wheel. Bain also had dropped out of the race.

Horn's chances for a top placing were fading fast. With about five laps to go, he disappeared from the breakaway. A few laps later he was not in the first three groups. In kermises, a race official will wave the bulk of the field off the course before the riders finish the full distance. If you're out of contention, you're out of the race. By the time

Horn finished, in around 19th position out of the 106 starters, traffic was already beginning to fill the course.

Horn told me he was coming off a five-day rest period and was

The course was opening to traffic by the time Horn finished.
Photo by Daniel Lee

preparing for an upcoming stage race. "I put myself in a good situation for the race but unfortunately couldn't finish it off," he said before devouring a goat-cheese-and-jelly sandwich after the race.

As we drove back to the Cycling Center after the kermis, Horn talked about what motivated him to put off his studies and career to pursue a pro contract: "I like the routine of racing and what it demands, obviously of my body but also of my character and my work habits." He talked about the need to be savvy as well as strong. "You can race for two hundred kilometers, but one mistake can cost your whole day."

Moerman saw great potential in Horn: "No doubt, he's more than pro-worthy already," he said. "By the end of this year, the guy should knock on the door for the real pro level." Horn's past results included third place at the 2009 USA Cycling Elite Road National Championships in Bend, Oregon. (He was fourth, but second-place finisher David Clinger was later disqualified after he failed a doping test.)

And just days after fading from the front of the kermis, Horn finished seventh in the Tweedaagse van de Gaverstreek, a two-day race for elite riders that scaled Oude Kwaremont—one of the Tour of Flanders's famed cobbled climbs—three times. Belgian cycling legend Johan Museeuw won the race in 1985.

Other results followed, including a third place in the Tour of Antwerp in Belgium and first place in the mountains and combined classifications in the Tour de Bourbourg-Watten in France.

Yet his 2010 season brought as much disappointment as triumph. In May, a virus ruined his form for some of the key races of the year. And in August and September, he battled a persistent cough. "I had good results but not as good as I expected," Horn said. "I think most riders feel this sort of disappointment pretty much every season. It's never quite as good as you want it to be . . . I've learned to take the bad luck in stride and to move on," Horn said.

But Belgium, especially West Flanders, was feeling like home. He's learning to speak more Dutch and French. He was planning on racing for the Geox-Fuji Test Team, which was affiliated with the professional Geox squad, for the coming season. Horn, though, was preparing for life beyond the bike. Barolo-Rizvi started studies for a PhD at Oxford University in England in fall 2010. Horn has a scholarship waiting at the University of Michigan Law School. He was planning on applying to other top law schools including Columbia, Harvard, Yale, and the University of Chicago. Whenever his racing career ended, Horn planned to pursue work in law and public service. "It's nice to know that I have great opportunities outside of cycling as well," he said.

Moerman talked about riders such as Horn with a certain level of pride: Whatever Horn's future in the sport holds, he has pushed himself to the brink of his dream. Moerman saw such success as being as much about mental attitude as physical strength and endurance.

Horn had learned to compete in, and not just try to finish, each race. Most Americans coming to the Cycling Center leave without pro contracts. Yet, Moerman said, most come in hoping they could become pros.

Moerman searched for a comparison. "If you've not been at the Grand Canyon, you cannot tell them how enormous the Grand Canyon is." In the same way, new riders may come in with impossibly high hopes. "Do they have the right expectations? No," Moerman said, before adding: "They have the right hopes."

Moerman, born in 1958, knows about such hopes. He played in the Belgian pro soccer league for five years, but seventeen broken bones in his feet and bum knees forced him to retire at the age of twenty-six. "I am not too cocky to admit that I was crying like a baby for days," he said. Moerman still carries the legacy of those injuries in his hobbled knees and swollen ankles.

A young American's journey to the Cycling Center begins with a load of paperwork, starting with an eighteen-page initial questionnaire. "Many days you will be tired and suffering like a beaten dog. Some days cycling will not even be fun anymore," reads the opening paragraph of the questionnaire. The document goes on to ask applicants basic questions about their height, weight, age, background in cycling, and family and educational histories. Then the questions probe ever deeper, including queries such as: "Did you ever have to share a room growing up?" "On a scale of 1 to 10, how healthy and well balanced is your daily diet?" "On a scale of 1 to 10, are you a good cook?" "How often do you check your resting pulse?" "How often do you check your weight?" "Do you do Pilates?" "Who do you feel cares about you as a person no matter how you do in cycling?" and "Do you think there is a big difference in the approach of doping in your country and most of Europe?"

Moerman then assembles a team of roughly twenty-five riders of varying ages, nationalities, and racing backgrounds from the 250 to 350 applications. The average length of stay at the center is four and a half months. Riders are evaluated for longer stays based on their performance and progress. "I do not know, and they do not know, how long they will last," he said.

New Cycling Center riders also visit bike-fit master Frans Vanmarcke soon after they arrive in Belgium. Vanmarcke's shop breathed Belgian cycling heritage: It was organized but not fancy, precise but not computerized. In fact, his fit shop didn't even have a computer. On this day in early April, Moerman accompanied Australian Fuji Test Team rider Trent Williams to Vanmarcke's small tidy home on the outskirts of Izegem. Vanmarcke was a thin elderly man with thick eyebrows, gray hair, and reading glasses. The window at his desk looked out to the tidy pond and fountain in his backyard. Inside, the shop was filled with bins of bike parts, bolts, and handmade devices to measure riders' limbs and trunks. A calendar featuring women in swimsuits was on display, as was the memorial service program for the late Belgian cycling star Frank Vandenbroucke, one of the many professional cyclists Vanmarcke had provided fitting services for over the years.

Bernard Moerman, right, talks with bike-fit expert Frans Vanmarcke.
Photo by Daniel Lee

Williams stood awkwardly wearing just his cycling bib shorts and socks as Vanmarcke inspected the young rider. He placed his hand on the backs of his knee, counted vertebrae, and measured across Williams's chest and the length of his arms. He asked Williams to march in place to see how his feet landed. He had Williams straddle a device used to measure leg length before pulling an adjustable metal bar upward into the young rider's crotch. "There's a bit of trust here," Williams said with an awkward smile. Vanmarcke studied the bottom of Williams's feet to see where the cleats should sit. He also checked and measured all of the angles on Williams's bike. All of this was recorded on paper.

After a pause came the verdict. "You have very long legs and in comparison short arms," Vanmarcke told Williams in Dutch, with Moerman translating. Vanmarcke said overall Williams's bike fit was good. But he saw problems. He wiggled the cleats on Williams's shoes to determine they were not sitting tightly enough in the pedals: a source of wasted power with every pedal stroke. And that wasn't all: "The handlebars have to come up like four centimeters." He said Williams was positioned too deep in the saddle, which was cutting blood off to his legs and making him uncomfortable. Vanmarcke flipped the stem on Williams's bike so it angled upward. That raised the handlebars, as Vanmarcke wanted, but it made the bike look less like a racing machine and more like a recreational touring bike. "That is so ugly," Williams said quietly. Perhaps, but finding the right bike position was vital to becoming efficient on the bike and avoiding overuse injuries. It's all part of the process of adapting to the longer international races.

Riders at the Cycling Center also received training manuals and other documents detailing Moerman's approach to life on and off the bike. It's a mix of practical tips and cycling philosophy.

On building a base of lower-intensity endurance training in the off season:

In building base-endurance NO PAIN NO GAIN is a stupid saying. If you look back at the results most of our riders got over the years you will see that they mostly had a consistent growth, month after month, year after year. This is because of their better and better base-endurance. It's like building a house.

On dressing properly for training:

In Belgium the combination of the cold, coastal moisture and the wind can be very dangerous, yes even devastating if you're not dressed right. Here it will only take 30 seconds to get sick because of not being dressed right. So 30 seconds can ruin 10 or more days . . . Do you know that humid air conducts heat up to 30 percent faster than dry air . . . ? Do you know that wind makes your body lose body heat much faster . . . ? Dress warmly.

On acting like a professional, on and off the bike:

The way you talk, the way you are dressed, the way you eat, the way you are organized, how clean your bike and clothing is, all this and more is part of your personal communication package. People will perceive all this a certain way and this way you create an image . . . Becoming a professional cyclist is a public job, your sponsors will pay you partly because your behavior, your image will help to enforce their company or product or service.

Yet riders have to experience some realities of Belgium for themselves. Thompson got sick after being caught in a rainstorm during a training ride two hours from the Cycling Center. His broken jaw, the flu, and a case of bronchitis kept Thompson from racing as much as he wanted. He passed much of his time in the garage and at races working as the Fuji Test Team mechanic. At times, he would head to

Bruges with teammates for a beer, or to the beach at Nieuwpoort to look at sailboats. He counted among his highlights in Belgium a fourth-place finish in a kermis in which he won 50 euros.

"It was a season full of setbacks, that's what it was. As soon as I got rolling I'd get injured or sick and have to take time off the bike," Thompson said. He did roughly thirty races in Belgium, fewer than he had hoped. But he had learned. He vividly described just where he wanted to ride in the pack: "You want to be at the front, but you don't want to be on the front. You want to be maybe fifteen guys back . . . It's like you're trying to surf a wave. There's only one spot on the crest of the wave that works."

For Addison Bain, the lessons of his first season in Belgium were all about learning to race—to be aggressive and attentive in the pack as opposed to simply struggling to hang on. His proudest moment of the season came in a summer kermis near Bruges in which he did not even finish, but instead crashed with just three kilometers to go. But before he hit the deck, he was attacking. He was fighting. "I was strong all day," Bain said. "I actually raced."

Moerman's assessment of Thompson and Bain's Belgian cycling baptism was part praise, part critique. On Thompson: "He has for sure much more potential but needs to learn to focus on being a bike racer full-time. Then we will see much more," Moerman said. Of Bain, he added: "Addison Bain's first experience is one where now he needs to decide how much more he wants to put in. I think he discovered that talent alone is not doing miracles. But the powerhouse he is can go far if he gets the right motivation."

Thompson returned home to Maryland in late summer to work as a bike mechanic at REI. Seeing his friends start careers, he started to think about graduate school in environmental studies. Bain returned from Belgium in the summer of 2010 and was working as a personal trainer in his native Minnesota. He was making plans to return to college in Missouri in the fall. Both, though, hoped to return to Belgium.

9

The Curious Case of Gregg Germer

Google searches led me to Gregg Germer in Oudenaarde, Belgium. In doing my initial research for this book, I typed combinations of words *kermesse* (an alternative spelling of *kermis*), *Belgium,* and *housing* into the Internet search engine. My goal was to find where young unproven American cyclists—those not connected with the national team in Izegem or even with Bernard Moerman's Cycling Center—might stay while racing in Belgium.

I clicked on the link for TheChainStay.com, one of Germer's websites. The Chain Stay was Germer's home and small business in Oudenaarde, a Flemish town near the Koppenberg and other famous cobbled climbs of the Flemish Ardennes. Germer offered a seven-room home designed to accommodate cyclists—a big kitchen, a living room with digital cable, heated bedrooms (not always the case in Belgium, he pointed out), a washer and dryer, and a large patio area for washing bikes. Germer, through his Chainring Tours business, also offered lodging for touring cyclists visiting to ride Belgian roads and watch professional races. He described himself as an ex-professional-racer and his wife, Holly, as a massage therapist and experienced cycling soigneur.

Germer's website also linked to his well-researched list of tips for newcomers wanting to live and race in Belgium.

On grocery shopping with a tight budget:

The best and cheapest stores to shop for food are Lidl and Aldi. Lidl has more name brands and a bit more variety, but the cost is just a little more. Aldi is the cheapest, but lacks variety at times . . .

On locating kermises:

> The place to find races is on the website of the Wieler Bond Vlaanderen. You can also buy the monthly Cyclink magazine to find races, but it's best to use the Internet as races times, dates and locations often change (I've gone to more than one scheduled race that was canceled because of using just the Cyclink).

Other Web pages revealed more stories about this Texan living in Belgium. GreggGermer.com was packed with photos of Germer in kermises. The site linked to shots of him racing for the Cycling Center in 2002 and 2003, and then of Germer competing for small Belgian professional teams in 2004, 2005, and 2007. He was a blond-haired, slightly stocky racer—fit with muscular legs but not the thin belly, arms, and sunken cheeks of a climber or stage racer. He looked like a sturdy built-low-to-the-ground sprinter. A kermis guy. Other photos showed slices of Flemish life: a portly man balancing a load of beer while riding a bike, or Germer and a friend raising large chalices of dark Belgian brews at an outdoor beer garden.

Germer was a guy who had stayed in Belgium after he stopped racing. He and his Belgian-Canadian wife were building their lives there. I was intrigued, not by his cycling successes—I had met much more accomplished cyclists in reporting this book—but instead by the apparent cultural transformation of this guy from Houston.

I clicked on the CONTACT button and sent Germer an email telling him about my book idea. I said I'd like to come to Oudenaarde to see him. A couple months after we exchanged emails I was on a train riding from Izegem to Oudenaarde. I looked out the window to see hills in the distance—the Flemish Ardennes.

After arriving at Oudenaarde station, I walked down the street looking for Germer. After a quick cell phone call, we connected. I looked up to see a blond guy in jeans and a gray sweater standing next to his car waving to me. I recognized him from the photos, although he was a now a little heavier.

Soon we made our way to the nearby Tour of Flanders Center, a museum known as the Centrum Ronde van Vlaanderen. A cycling fan's visit to the Tour of Flanders museum in Oudenaarde is a delightful small-town experience similar to a baseball fan savoring a trip to the Baseball Hall of Fame in Cooperstown, New York. Germer took a photo of me with Belgian cycling legend Freddy Maertens,

Gregg Germer. Photo by Daniel Lee

who works at the museum. Maertens met guests and even collected their money and processed their credit cards. After paying our admission, Germer and I ventured through the exhibits, where we watched children riding stationary bikes designed to simulate riding on cobblestones. We looked at a photo of a lone soldier by his bicycle on a muddy Flemish road during World War I. We saw Eddy Merckx's bicycle and the support car for his legendary Flandria Team. Germer translated signs from Dutch into English for me.

But we spent most of our time talking over espresso in the museum's brasserie. Germer told me how he got into cycling after his family moved from New Orleans to Houston when he was about to start the seventh grade. His uncle took Germer and his younger brother to the Alkek Velodrome in Houston, and Germer had found his sport. After he graduated from high school in 1999 at the age of seventeen, he enrolled in the University of Houston. He later switched to Collin Community College in the Dallas area. Germer's dad and uncle were engineers, but cycling had become more important than class work. He said school was a distraction from cycling, and from his lofty goal of becoming a winner of the green-points jersey—the honor given to the winner of the points classification in the Tour de France. At nineteen, Germer left Texas and traveled to South Africa to stay with a friend's family for six months. In early 2002, the twenty-year-old Germer arrived in Belgium—specifically at the Cycling Center, directed by Bernard Moerman.

Germer, sitting with me in the Tour of Flanders museum eight years after his arrival in Belgium, seemed to have lost none of his idealism.

I asked him, "Why Belgium?"

"For me Belgium, it's the hardest road there is. It is the World Series. There is nothing harder for the type of rider I wanted to be than here," Germer said. "For me, watching grainy videos of Belgium and hard men covered in mud, just duking it out kilometer after kilometer, and coming back with that look of pure agony, it's a pure thing."

About a month into his Belgian adventure, Germer himself tasted the harshness of the sport. In a race, trying to rejoin the pack after falling behind on a climb, he crashed into the back of a team vehicle. He broke his collarbone and was out of competition for eight weeks.

Yet Germer, with pins holding his collarbone together, was back on the indoor trainer three days after the crash riding up to twenty hours a week.

Moerman of the Cycling Center took notice. "He impressed me the way he was getting over that as a rookie," Moerman said. "At that moment, I thought he had good potential." Germer went back to racing, but by the next season his relationship with Moerman was deteriorating. Germer—who said he paid around $3,200 to spend the season at the Cycling Center in 2003—wanted to ride in races for himself, not in support of other riders, as he said Moerman asked him to do.

Moerman saw an American lacking the patience required for developing cycling talent. In an American's dictionary, he told me, the word *patience* is crossed out in red with the word *instant* written in instead. He also saw Germer's expectations as a little too high.

Germer in 2003 didn't record stellar results on the road. Away from the bike, though, he was displaying a different set of skills. He loved to write. He also showed business instincts, lining up a new sponsorship deal for the Cycling Center. Moerman advised him to find another career. "I told him you are not a rider; you could be an excellent writer. The way he writes things, the way he could get sponsorship going, he has a big skill for that."

Eventually, Moerman kicked Germer out.

Germer returned to Texas, angry but not ready to give up on cycling. He trained and worked part-time in his mom's antiques business, helping her sell merchandise on eBay. He took the roughly $5,000 set aside for his college and used it for cycling. He bought a power meter for training.

Yet Germer also kept writing. He crafted a short novel, *Cobblestone Dreams,* about fictional young bike racer Andy Bennett, who left college to race in Belgian kermises. Germer drew from his own experiences. Andy loved Belgian chocolate pastries, *chocoladekoeken,* just like Germer. In the book, Andy was confused by the sign ANDERE RICHTING posted among other signs pointing to towns in Flanders. He assumed Andere Richting was a town, only to find out it means "other direction." It's the way the Flemish navigate: either go toward a town, or go the other direction.

Yet there were differences. Fictional Andy's parents saw his bike racing as a distraction from his need to find a real career. Germer said his parents were always supportive.

He self-published *Cobblestone Dreams* under the fictional name Brent Bender, not wanting his own name attached to the book in case he turned pro and people would search the story believing it was autobiographical. Germer also would write dispatches about his life in Belgium for the website PezCyclingNews.com. He taught himself graphic design and website development.

In his search for a team for the 2004 season, Germer called Frans Assez, a well-known former Belgian pro and team director, about a room to rent. "No problem," Assez said. Rent was 250 euros a month.

Germer called back in December to confirm his room, and Assez said, "Yeah, yeah, no problem." Then Assez asked Germer, "How old are you?" Germer replied, "Twenty-three."

"You want to ride pro?" Assez asked.

And with that, Germer—perhaps brought on to help fulfill rider age requirements for small pro teams—joined the Flanders Pro Cycling Team. He was paid no salary. He lived in a small apartment above a row of shops and a Chinese restaurant six kilometers north of Oudenaarde.

He'd race three years for pro teams in Belgium—2004–2005 and 2007—never earning more than 300 euros a month and a free place to stay. In 2006, he searched unsuccessfully for a contract with a pro team in America. He married Holly and returned to Belgium, racing mostly kermises but also some bigger events. Once looking down between his legs during an attack, he saw the gold shoes of 2004 Olympic champion and Italian cycling star Paolo Bettini whirling on the pedals nearby.

Gregg Germer, second from right (foreground), in 2005 in Belgium.
Photo courtesy Gregg Germer

Germer had never made enough money to truly be considered a pro, yet he had experienced the pro cyclist's life. By 2007, he saw entrepreneurial opportunities in Belgium. He started subletting the spare rooms in his rented house. He retired from racing and started working in an air-duct factory and as a bartender in an Irish pub. Eventually, Germer and his wife bought a home—the front of the home a converted butcher shop—to set up the Chain Stay guesthouse and Chainring Tours business.

William "Booey" Hottenstein, then an seventeen-year-old, was among the young racers to stay at Germer's house during the 2010 racing season. Hottenstein, from Kingston near the Scranton Wilkes-

Barre area of northern Pennsylvania, had raced as a youngster before taking several years off to, as he put it, be a teenager and play baseball. He started to ride again after returning from a trip to northern Spain to study Spanish in 2009. During the trip, he had caught a bus to southern France to see the Tour de France and Lance Armstrong pass by. That trip, along with an arm injury, made cycling an exciting alternative to baseball.

After a busy schedule of junior races, Hottenstein headed to Belgium with a team that stayed at Germer's Chain Stay house. As with so many young American racers before, he struggled. Full of nervous energy and a desire to prove himself, he spent too much time in the wind. He took a corner too fast and went off course. He bonked before the race ended. He didn't prepare to drink enough water during a race to stay hydrated—saved by Germer showing up with bottles to hand off.

Germer also counseled Hottenstein on how to deal with the physical and intimidating nature of junior racing in Belgian. Riders will scream, with an arm angrily flailing, for a nervous rider to work at the front of a group while the Belgian enjoys the draft, Hottenstein had learned. A Belgian may grab an unsuspecting rider's hip to sling himself forward while the newbie hurdles backward through the pack. A nervous or uncomfortable rider is easy prey.

Germer told Hottenstein that *Don't fuck with me!* is a universal phrase. "If I said it with enough oomph, even a non-English-speaker would understand," Hottenstein remembered Germer telling him. In a race the next day, one rider predictably flipped out: He screamed and threw his hand around and moved closer to Hottenstein.

In response, Hottenstein lifted an arm in anger. "Don't fuck with me, buddy!" screamed Hottenstein, looking as crazy as possible. "Don't fucking fuck with me!"

The Belgian shut up and backed off.

Germer helped Hottenstein in other ways. He nudged him to be more organized. Hottenstein often would be scurrying around the house trying to find a lost glove or arm warmer shortly before a race. Germer advised him to pack his bag and prepare the night before— set out water bottles, pins, and everything else needed to eliminate unneeded stress.

Germer's panache for organization is evident from his websites. So is his love of Belgian culture.

As we sat in the Tour of Flanders museum talking, our espressos long gone, Germer told me that he gets homesick for Belgium when he's back in the States. He said he loves the slightly slower pace of life. He loves being able to ride his bike the short distances to the bakery, grocery store, or train station.

Before we stopped talking, I pulled my copy of his *Cobblestone Dreams* book from my bag and asked Germer to sign it. I had bought it online and enjoyed reading it before my trip to Belgium. I quickly tucked the book back into my bag before we then left the museum and headed to Germer's home. He then dropped me off at the train station for my journey back to Izegem.

I settled into my seat on the train and grabbed the book from my bag. I flipped to the first page and read Germer's inscription: "Always keep the passion of the ride with you and the bike will take you wherever you will."

10

Back in the USA

"I'm up in the balcony to your right," said Daniel Holloway, his words transmitting from his cell phone to mine. Sitting in the bar in the cavernous lobby of the Sheraton Philadelphia City Center Hotel, I turned and looked up to see Holloway—recognizable with his red hair, dark-framed glasses, and red, white, and black Team Bissell jersey—waving from a couple of floors above. We were meeting up in a hotel lobby buzzing with riders and team officials getting ready for the next day's 156-mile TD Bank Philadelphia International Cycling Championship.

The race, simply known as "Philly," was one of those few events that made pro bike racing seem like a major sport in the United States. The one-day race had been run each June since 1985.

Holloway made his way down the escalator through the lobby to my table in the hotel bar. The last time I had seen him was in a much different setting: in the frigid rain in Belgium as he rode with Taylor Phinney at the Triptyque des Monts et Châteaux (detailed in chapter 3). Holloway raised his arms in triumph back in the pack as he watched Team USA teammate Phinney take a stage win. Since then, Holloway had been racing for Team Bissell on the US domestic circuit in events including those that mixed professionals and amateurs such as the Sea Otter Classic in California and the Joe Martin Stage Race in Arkansas.

In May, he lined up against the stars of his sport—Lance Armstrong, George Hincapie, Levi Leipheimer, Tom Boonen, Fabian Cancellara, and Mark Cavendish—at the Tour of California. Having never raced at such a high level, he was nervous and unsure of his fitness. He showed his potential as a field sprinter by placing thirteenth in stage 4 behind winner Francesco Chicchi of Italy. But the next stage he was forced to quit the race after hitting his knee in a high-speed crash that also forced the abandonment of Armstrong.

Philly was his next shot on a big stage. "Philly is really known as a sprinters race, but it's been won from a breakaway. I came here for results, but I also came here for experience," Holloway told me. The previous year, in 2009, he had launched a solo attack in the opening miles of the Philly race. For roughly three hours, he rode alone. He drew energy from the crowds on the Manayunk Wall, a steep house-lined climb the riders tackle each circuit through the neighborhood of Manayunk. "The Wall," as it is known, has become US cycling's version of the Wrigley Field bleachers—a place for people to party.

"The atmosphere on the wall is crazy, so loud and positive that you can't hear yourself breathe," Holloway said. During his 2009 attack, he wore his Team USA cycling kit, which brought spirited chants of "USA! USA! USA!" each time Holloway labored up the hill. Holloway loved hearing those cheers from the loud Philly sports fans.

Holloway's solo breakaway eventually was caught, but it took much of the race because the pack rode at a pace slow enough that the elite women racers of the Liberty Classic—who started after the men—caught and passed the men's peloton. In the end, German sprinter Andre Greipel won the 2009 edition by outsprinting what was left of the main pack.

Race co-founder David Chauner has seen a shift in tactics in his race since it began a quarter century before. "What's happened is the riders have learned how to ride the course a lot better than they used to," said Chauner, a two-time Olympic cyclist who heads the Pro Cycling Tour, the Pennsylvania-based business that organizes the Philly race. "The teams are really planning tactics. They're not so stretched or blown out by the wall. Lots of times it comes down to the breakaway that has been dangling for a long time and it's reeled in."

Indeed, Philly offered riders and team directors something that was not common in US cycling: the chance to race year after year what was pretty much the same course—the 14.4-mile circuit that runs from the Benjamin Franklin Parkway, along Kelly Drive next to the Schuylkill River, to the Manayunk Wall, and back downtown. For more than a generation, Philly had been a constant in an ever-changing US domestic circuit.

In contrast, Europe's great races date back generations to the dawn of the transportation revolution brought by the development of the bicycle and automobile. The famed cobblestone classic Paris–Roubaix started in 1896, the Tour de France in 1903, and the Tour of Flanders in 1913.

While in Belgium in the spring of 2010, I picked up a copy of the English-language weekly newspaper *Flanders Today*. In the main story, headlined "Cobblestone Heroism," writer Anja Otte opened her essay on the Tour of Flanders by telling of how the sound of helicopters hovering above reminded her of Belgium's greatest race: the whirling rotors meant the riders were near. "Like many people, this reminds me of my childhood, when every family gathering seemed to include watching one or another bicycle race," Otte wrote.

America's road-racing scene lacks anything close to that grandeur. But Chauner had come as close as any race promoter at linking his event to Philly's wider sports culture. Still, it was interesting to note that some of the loudest cheers I heard during the 2010 race were in response to a race official riding on the back of a motorcycle holding up a whiteboard with the words GO FLYERS! written on it. The NHL's Philadelphia Flyers were in the Stanley Cup finals. US pro bike races, tied to sponsors' marketing strategies and budgets, typically vanish after a few years—a huge frustration for US cycling's racers and fans alike. In the 1970s and '80s, Colorado had the Red Zinger and Coors Classic stage race. In 1989 and 1990, East Coast cycling fans were treated to the Tour de Trump (yes, a stage race just for Donald). That became the Tour DuPont, but it, too, was gone by the mid-1990s.

More recently the Tour de Georgia and Tour of Missouri have come and gone.

Philly, though, became a common link for most of the famous American cyclists of the modern era: Greg LeMond, Andy Hampsten, Alexi Grewal, Davis Phinney, Bobby Julich, Chris Horner, George Hincapie, Lance Armstrong, and Tyler Farrar are among those who have raced the circuit through the City of Brotherly Love.

My fascination with the Philly race began in 1987 when I was a teenager feeding a newly discovered love for bike racing by road-tripping to the race. In 1988, I met Hampsten fresh off his legendary ride over the snowy Gavia Pass on his way to become the first and only American to win the Giro d'Italia.

In 1989, my buddies and I watched Greg LeMond—still looking for the form he'd had before his 1987 hunting accident—wearing blue jeans and tinkering with his bike before the race in Philly. The very next month, LeMond would famously beat Frenchman Laurent Fignon by eight seconds to win the Tour de France.

In 1993, as I was finishing grad school, I became an employee of the Philly race—signing a four-month contract position that paid a princely sum of $300 a week to work as a communications assistant for Chauner. It was a good year. Lance Armstrong, in his first full year as a pro, launched an attack on the Manayunk Wall to win the US pro championship. With the victory, he also won the "$1 million Triple Crown"—winning Philly as well as earlier races in Pittsburgh and West Virginia.

While Philly has survived, it also has gone through many changes since 1985. A women's race, the Liberty Classic, was added in 1996. But there also have been downsizings. The race used to be part of a week of racing, with smaller buildup events in nearby Lancaster, Trenton, or Reading. The race—long known as the CoreStates US Pro Championship—also lost its status as crowning the US road champion after 2005. In 2009, the race was almost canceled because of sponsorship woes.

Author, then fresh-faced and bright-eyed, with Andy Hampsten
at Philly in 1988.

Author's prized Philly race event pass from 1993.

In short, the Philly race has had stamina that would impress even
Rocky Balboa.

The 2010 race provided more reminders how, if given time, bike
racing can be embraced by mainstream American sports fans. On the

Manayunk Wall, a group of burly young men in NBA jerseys (probably some of the same dudes who had cheered on Holloway's solo breakaway the year before) partied hard in front of the "watering hole"—a makeshift shower spraying water onto the course to cool off the riders, and themselves. They chanted "USA!" "USA!" "USA!" "USA!" for US National Team riders and "SWE-DEN!" "SWE-DEN!" SWE-DEN!" for the mostly blond Swedish national team.

At one point, two party boys hoping to start the wave tried to enlist the help of a cigarette-smoking, tough-guy-looking Philly cop. The square-jawed officer was not about to join in the frivolity: "See those girls over there?" asked the cop, pointing toward two young sundress-wearing women. "I don't think the all-guy thing is workin' for ya." A few moments later, the two party boys were doing the wave with the young women.

The riders, of course, miss out on such festivities. (Although riders—particularly those in doomed breakaways or out of contention—at times join in by raising an imaginary beer can for a drink as they pedal up "The Wall," an interaction that delights fans partying on porches of nearby homes.)

The California-based Jelly Belly Cycling Team Presented by Kenda—in its eleventh year, a mainstay on the US domestic scene—had designated veteran Mike Friedman as its race leader. Friedman's job was to stay fresh for the final ten kilometers of the race and go for the sprint win or a late-race attack, depending on the situation. Teammate Bernard van Ulden's task for the race was simply to stay close to Friedman to keep him fueled up and out of the wind. The sturdily built five-foot-ten, 170-pound Friedman, nicknamed "Meatball," was a natural leader for Jelly Belly. Born in 1982, Friedman had accomplished much in cycling: He was a member of the 2008 Olympic team and had ridden in Europe with the Garmin-Slipstream team in grueling races such as Paris–Roubaix, Tour of Flanders, and Ghent Wevelgem.

Teammate Kiel Reijnen's job was to get in breakaways so the team

Fun times on the Manayunk Wall. Photo by Darrell Parks,
darrellparks.com

did not have to expend extra energy at the front of the pack chasing
down attacks in which the team was not represented. Reijnen was
feeling "over-raced" after competing in the Tours of Thailand, Korea,
and California in April and May, but he also knew his duties were
confined to the first half of the race. He wasn't expected to finish.

Reijnen and Canadian teammate Will Routley followed multiple
attacks in the first thirty kilometers of racing. Reijnen eventually
made it into a breakaway with Routley.

"My legs are shit today," Reijnen told Routley as the group crested
"The Wall" partway through the race. "How are you feeling?"

Routley said he still felt good, so Reijnen did what he could to
help maintain a good pace and keep Routley out of the wind. Reijnen said he was eager to sacrifice for Routley after the Canadian had
done the same for him in earlier races. Routley eventually launched
a solo attack off the front of the breakaway—a move that garnered
plenty of exposure for Jelly Belly from the live race announcers and

on TV, much to the delight of the jelly bean maker and the team's German-based bike sponsor, Focus. Reijnen soon was out of the race cheering from the sidelines, as he put it.

The 2010 race was, though, shaping up in vintage Philly fashion: the sprinters' teams gobbling all attacks. Team Bissell's Holloway had made the front selection. So did Jelly Belly's Friedman. But it was again foreign-born riders in the best position for the final sprint down Benjamin Franklin Parkway. In fact, those faithful Philly fans have not often had the opportunity to yell "USA! USA!" at the finish. From 1985 through 2010, just eleven of the twenty-six winners in Philly were Americans—an embarrassing statistic considering that for twenty-one years the race also served as the US pro championship.

Fresh off his Giro d'Italia stage win, Australian Matthew Goss of HTC-Columbia prevailed in a field sprint of thirty-four riders into a stiff head-cross wind to win Philly in a time of 6:15:46. Peter Sagan, a twenty-year-old Slovakian on Liquigas, was second. Norwegian Alexander Kristoff of BMC placed third. The highest-placed American was Shawn Milne of Team Type 1 in tenth. Jelly Belly's Michael Friedman sprinted to eleventh place, followed by Holloway in twelfth.

For Holloway, finishing in contention for the win in the front group of thirty-four after 156 miles of racing was a good sign. "I got better and better as the day went on," he said. "I think the longer races suit me well, and I'm really starting to fully enjoy them."

The 2010 race was a crucial one for Holloway. He had turned twenty-three in May—not old by cycling standards, but he was getting too old to be part of the US National Development Team. With no more trips to Izegem in his future, Holloway was aiming his career in two possible directions in the coming years. The first goal was to win enough on the domestic circuit to land a contract with a Pro Tour team focused on the big races of Europe. If that didn't happen, he'd look to still race domestically but also compete regularly in European six-day track races in the late-fall and winter months. "I have two pretty solid options. If one doesn't work out then hopefully the other one does," Holloway said.

US domestic racing is not a road to riches. It may not even provide enough income to move riders out of their parents' home and into a modest apartment. According to multiple discussions with racing insiders, pro racers on the US circuit may make zero in pay—basically, their pay may go for travel. They are riding for the opportunity to be professional cyclists and, hopefully, pedal their way to better deals. Others may make $8,000 to $12,000 a year; better riders, $25,000 to $30,000. An elite few riders earn $80,000 on the US circuit. Prize money or start fees can boost those numbers by around $20,000 a year. Typically, riders have to buy their own health insurance. Many buy coverage through USA Cycling. Some buy bare-bones catastrophic plans with high deductibles. The federal health care reform passed under President Obama allowing young people to stay on their parents' health plan until the age of twenty-six would give riders another option. Dr. Dawn Richardson, an emergency medicine physician and former cycling team doctor, said she had counseled riders on how to navigate the complexities of the US health care system: If you have $100, go to the urgent care center; if you're broke, go to the ER.

Pro cyclists do rack up frequent-flier miles, as well as driving miles. Danny Van Haute, team director for Jelly Belly, noted that from February through October the riders' schedule averages out to roughly two weeks at home, two weeks on the road. Accommodations can vary from five-star hotels on an Asian racing trip, to comfortable hotels such as the Sheraton in Philadelphia, to host families. The team returns to some host families year after year because of their hospitality and ability to feed entire hungry cycling teams. But Van Haute also pulled his team from homes and placed them in a motel after four or five riders were cramped into a family's camper trailer, or a host family refused to provide accommodations for the team's two female massage therapists.

Even if the lifestyle isn't glamorous, the competition for contracts is still fierce. Sometimes it's as much about demonstrating strength and guts as it is about specific results. "I know plenty of guys who have gotten contracts off of nothing more than being in a good move or following a really hard attack . . . being the ones who had the strength to do it," Reijnen said.

Tight budgets are not surprising given that American cycling lacks the basic revenue sources of other pro sports—ticket sales and TV money. The pay among bigger-budget teams competing primarily in Europe is better, typically starting around $50,000 a year. Established European-based pros can make into six figures, with the top stars of the sport earning $1 million or more, including income from endorsements. "Financially, it makes a lot more sense. It's much more of a profession," said Ted King, a New Hampshire native who made a steady progression through the sport. He raced in collegiate cycling as a student at Vermont's Middlebury College, competed with the US Development Team in Europe, and turned pro on the domestic circuit before joining the Cervélo Test Team in 2009 to focus on Europe. King echoed other American pros who now spend much of their season in Europe in talking affectionately about the fun and camaraderie of the domestic circuit, but also expressing a desire to prove themselves in Europe. "I don't want to discredit American cycling, but I think of American cycling as a lot guys coming out of college, and it's sort of a bachelor lifestyle. You go to the race and have fun and then go home and kick in Boulder." (Boulder, of course, is the earthy Colorado college town that has long been a cycling hotbed.)

As a domestic pro from 2006 to 2008, King garnered results such as a stage win at the Joe Martin Stage Race in Arkansas in 2008, or wearing the King of the Mountains jersey in the Tour of Georgia the same year. "There's a great thing happening here," he said of US racing. "But Europe is where I want to be." King, born in 1983, established his qualification for international racing by completing the Giro d'Italia in 2009 and 2010.

"What is your next immediate goal?" I asked King. "Is the Tour de France out there?" It's a question he had heard before. American riders can build successful European careers without competing in the world's most famous race. But the Tour is the one race almost everyone in America knows. "Racing the Tour would be huge," he said. "You come back to America and people ask you all the time, 'Oh, you race professional cycling. That's exciting. Have you ever done the Tour?' People don't understand why you haven't. So just being able to say yes, that'd be really nice."

Team BMC's Brent Bookwalter, born in 1984, is a rider who accomplished just that in 2010.

The Michigan native gained broad attention in the cycling world after the Stage 1 time trial in the 2010 Giro d'Italia, where he finished second behind British star Bradley Wiggins over an 8.4-kilometer course through Amsterdam. Bookwalter's strong debut was part of a three-year progression of steadily taking on more top-level European races. In 2008, he competed in the Tour de Romandie, a weeklong stage race in Switzerland, along with a few other European races and a crowded schedule of US events. In 2009, he spent about half the season in Europe. In 2010, he spent most of the season in Europe. In fact, Bookwalter shared an apartment with Ted King in Girona, Spain.

Participating in one of cycling's Grand Tours—the Giro d'Italia, Tour de France, or Vuelta a España—is a milestone achievement for a young rider: three weeks of racing against top competition. For Bookwalter at the 2010 Giro, not looking too far ahead was the challenge. Don't flip ahead through the "race bible"—the book given to each rider that outlines each day's route, distance, and climbs, which totaled 3,418 kilometers (more than 2,120 miles) in twenty-one stages. "The first day and the first week you're suffering so much, you think, *Wow, this can't go on. I can't keep doing this.* But then you look at the profiles and the stages to come and you realize it's not going to get any easier." Yet Bookwalter did endure, finishing in ninety-fifth place overall as he rode in support of Australian BMC leader Cadel Evans, who finished fifth, 3:27 behind winner Ivan Basso of Italy.

After the Giro, Bookwalter returned home to Athens, Georgia. Two weeks after the Giro, he was experiencing sensations new to him as a bike racer. Fatigue, certainly, but he also had mental demons. He felt proud for having pushed himself harder than ever before, but he also described feeling desensitized and understimulated on his bike. "I felt strong," Bookwalter said. "I never felt really bad, but I also never felt really good."

It was around this time that BMC Racing Team Chief Director John Lelangue and President Jim Ochowitz first approached Bookwalter about riding the Tour de France. They asked him, *How do you feel? Can you do it? Do you want to do it?*

"I was as honest as I could be with them, which is a little awkward because you hear about these other teams where guys are just fighting to the death for Tour spots," Bookwalter said. "They say it's the highlight of their career if they get selected to do the Tour, and here I am hemming and hawing about it, like 'I don't know.'" In the end, BMC wanted him to do the Tour, and Bookwalter seized the opportunity. He had been scheduled to head back to Europe to do the Tour of Austria, but instead he headed to the Netherlands for the July 3 start of the Tour de France in Rotterdam.

The first stage, a 223.5-kilometer road race from Rotterdam to Brussels, provided an instant lesson in the intensity of the Tour. Bookwalter thought he had done some stressful races before, including France's cobblestone classic Paris–Roubaix and the Giro. But Stage 1 trumped them all. The peloton whizzed through Dutch and Belgian towns with the roads lined with thousands of spectators. Fans jumped in and out of the roads as they watched for the pack. Riders elbowed one another for position. Beer bottles in the road created an extra hazard. Brakes slammed. Riders crashed around him. "There was only like ten kilometers of the course that wasn't completely lined by fans. And when I say *lined,* I mean this almost deafening rain-

Brent Bookwalter. Photo by Tim de Waele

bow-vision tunnel of noise and color. On top of that, everyone is fresh. Everyone has everything to lose, as well as everything to gain," Bookwalter said. "The nervousness and the energy and the stress of the peloton that day . . . I burned a lot of mental and emotional matches that day."

The Tour de France is a massive display of the mental fortitude of its participants. Even the days where the pack finished together in a sprint were exhausting, according to Bookwalter. The pack is glued together in the collective determination of its individual parts, each rider willing himself onto the wheel in front. "It's frustrating to hear it commented on sometimes because the difficulty gets underplayed: 'Oh, they're just rolling along in the pack,'" he said. "But you don't realize these are like two hundred of the strongest physical and mental competitors in the world, and they're just feeling it together."

And just riding is not enough. As a domestique, Bookwalter's role was to look after Team BMC leader Cadel Evans—keep him out of the wind and supplied with bottles. He'd accompany Evans back to the medical car behind the pack and pedal in the wind as Evans hung on to the car talking. If Evans wanted to talk to another team's leader, Bookwalter would shepherd the Australian around the pack to find him and sit out in the wind while Evans had his conversation.

Yet Bookwalter learned to cope, just as he had at the Giro. The Tour became a routine of survival. Finish the stage, take a shower on the bus, and get to the hotel to rest because every minute of recovery counts. Food. Massages. Ice baths to beat the heat. After the first few days, Bookwalter lacked the energy to read much, listen to music, or even open his laptop computer. Some days, the team soigneurs would bring his suitcase to the hotel, but it would sit unopened. He'd simply live out of his race bag. The soigneurs would do his daily laundry and he'd wear the same thing the next day. A simple two-hundred-yard walk from the finish line to the team bus could take fifteen minutes because of throngs of fans. "Having someone ask for your water bottle and being so excited that they are jumping up and down or almost shaking or screaming at you for it, that's an experience you don't get in the US," Bookwalter said.

Bookwalter finished the 2010 Tour in 147th place, one of eight Americans to start and six to finish the race.

The US domestic racing circuit seemed a world away from the Tour de France. But it can be a springboard to launch riders on to successful European careers.

Kiel Reijnen's name is Dutch, and he still has family in Europe, but his is not a cycling family. He grew up on Bainbridge Island, in Washington State's Puget Sound area. It was there that Reijnen discovered cycling and a healthy respect for rain. Early on in his racing, as he competed on bikes with out-of-date downtube shifters, Reijnen said he was envious of kids with high-end equipment from bike-racing families. Yet his humble start in the sport soon became a matter of pride: "You know that's what you wanted, otherwise you wouldn't have tried so damn hard." He moved to Boulder to study mechanical engineering at the University of Colorado. He raced in collegiate competitions and with the US National Development Team and the Cycling Center in Europe.

In 2008, Jelly Belly team director Van Haute offered Reijnen a shot at pro racing. Over the next two and a half years, he became a top performer for the team.

Reijnen's 2010 season was not designed around the short criterium races that populate the US calendar, but rather around big stage races such as the Tour of California and marquee events including Philly and the US Professional Road Championship. He also performed well on Jelly Belly's racing forays into Asia, including winning the weeklong Tour of Thailand and placing fifth in the nine-stage Tour of Korea, which was won by teammate Michael Friedman.

Reijnen—despite being frustrated by his amateur stint racing in Europe with the US Development Team and Bernard Moerman's Cycling Center—is longing to compete in the great races of Europe. For 2011, he's signed with Team Type 1, a US team—founded in 2004 by cyclists with diabetes—that upgraded to UCI Pro Continental status as part of a drive to compete in some of Europe's biggest races.

"I loved it. I loved the bad weather. I loved the patterns, the misery, the whole thing," Reijnen said. Yet he also talked about loving the US circuit—of racing with friends, of relying on his ability to win prize money, of his time with Jelly Belly. "I hope that Europe is what I want it to be."

Van Haute would have loved to keep Reijnen in the Jelly Belly fold, but is happy to see him get that European opportunity. Reijnen has the tools, Van Haute said. He knows how to read races. He knows how to ride in the diagonal echelons that form on windswept European roads. At five-foot-nine and 138 pounds, Reijnen's a climber who is not afraid to mix it up in a field sprint. According to Van Haute, he also understands a pro cyclist's role as a human advertisement for his sponsor. He's game to do radio interviews on race day or to show up for a sponsor event when asked at the last minute.

But then Van Haute added that Reijnen likely will face an adjustment to European racing. The races are longer. He has yet to race challenging terrain like the Alps day after day against top pros. He'll be far from his Boulder, Colorado, home in Italy for many weeks at a time. "He's going to take probably a year or another two years to get experience under his belt before he starts producing there," Van Haute said.

For Holloway, the twelfth place in Philly in June was a sign of better things to come. In August, Holloway won the US pro criterium title in the Chicago suburb of Glencoe. Never mind that he placed fourth overall in the race—behind winner David Veilleux of Canada, along with an Australian and an Italian—the important thing was that Holloway was the first American to cross the line in the US Pro Criterium Championship. He jutted his arms skyward in victory just the same.

"I didn't have the superstar season that I was hoping for. I was expecting to put my hands up a little more," said Holloway, before adding, "It just kind of shows I can win bike races when it comes down to a pressure situation."

For 2011, Holloway signed with the Kelly Benefits Strategies cycling team. It's back to the domestic racing circuit, looking for that next moment to shine.

Ponytails in the Peloton

Sinead Miller was easy to pick out of the pack during the 57.6-mile TD Bank Liberty Classic in Philadelphia. Each lap I'd look for the tall, slender nineteen-year-old wearing tall black socks on her thin tan legs with a long blond ponytail fluttering in the wind behind her helmet. What's more, she usually was well positioned near the front of the peloton as she worked for her Peanut Butter & Co. team leader, sprinter Shelley Olds of California.

Miller, riding the elite women's race in Philadelphia for the first time, was given classic domestique duties for the day. She rode near the front to nullify other teams' moves. She maneuvered herself to keep Olds out of the wind. By the end of racing on a hot, windy June day, Miller had helped position Olds in the front group of twenty-two for the final sprint down Benjamin Franklin Parkway. Olds—a five-foot-two, 120-pound power-bolt of a sprinter—was particularly mindful of German sprint star Ina-Yoko Teutenberg, who had already won the Liberty Classic three times.

The TD Bank Liberty Classic ran as a race within a race—the men's field competed on the same course, on the same day. The women would start their competition just after the men and contest four laps of the 14.4-mile circuit, including four trips up the Manayunk Wall. It was a chance for the women to race before a big crowd in a big city. As Olds, Teutenberg, and the others wound up their sprint, they were—at least for that moment—the center of attention in Philadelphia.

Olds, an accomplished track cyclist used to tactical sprints, pounced early in an attempt to negate Teutenberg's powerful finishing kick. Yet Olds had jumped too soon, allowing Teutenberg time to recover and overtake her for the win. The sturdy German threw both arms skyward in celebration, almost losing control as her bike shook from a gust of wind.

Soon, the 28 women who made up what was left of the main chase field sprinted in, with Miller taking 3rd in the group and 25th over-all of 119 starters—a placing that earned her the prize for the race's best finisher under twenty-three years old. Olds was impressed by the result coming after so much work earlier in the race. "Sinead's job was done at that point, having worked harder than anyone in the entire race to get us to this point," she said.

Miller was with Olds and Teutenberg in the media tent for post-race interviews soon after the race. Still a few days from her twenti-eth birthday, Miller—the Pittsburgh girl who started cycling by bumping elbows with boys at the local BMX track—had arrived as one of the new stars of women's racing.

I had been following Miller through the race and was eager to talk with her. I knew her talent well—she raced as part of the highly re-garded cycling team at Marian University in Indianapolis. Miller also was in Izegem with the women's US National Team while I was in Belgium. What's more, she grew up near Pittsburgh competing (against the guys) in the Allegheny Cycling Association's weekly train-ing races. I, too, had lived near Pittsburgh growing up and had raced with the same club.

Miller cracked open a can of Diet Coke as I approached her after the Philadelphia race. I remarked that surely after a tough race she could enjoy a real sugar-filled Coke; she replied that she simply pre-ferred Diet Coke. Her thoughts on the day bubbled up like the fizz in her soft drink. "I didn't realize it was going to be this hot," she said. "It was brutal." She added that the crazies on the Manayunk Wall helped keep her going: "I couldn't even hear myself think going up that wall—it was so motivating to get up there, the adrenaline pumping!"

Another writer in the media tent held out a recorder and started asking Miller questions as I took out my camera to take her photo. Miller, talking to the writer, quickly stopped, looked directly at me, and flashed an exuberant smile before returning to her conversation. She seemed to soak up this moment of being part of big-time women's racing.

In fact, 2010 would become a breakout season for Miller. Just weeks after her performance in Philadelphia, she captured national championships in the road race and time trial for women under age twenty-three. In July, she rode as part of the US National Team in Italy's Giro Donne (the women's Giro), helping teammate Mara Abbott become the first American to win the women's Tour of Italy. Olds capped off the historic race by sprinting to victory in the final stage.

Miller was living her dream: She was a standout chemistry and math major at Marian University, a small Catholic school in Indianapolis that supports top cyclists with scholarships and flexible schedules. She raced for Team USA and for the trendy new trade team in women's cycling, Peanut Butter & Co. Twenty12. She was training with more structure and intensity than ever.

Miller was a product of her own talent and determination and of women's increased involvement in sports, but also of hyper-involved parents. Her goal is to compete in the 2012 Olympics and also to make her living—at least for a while—as a cyclist. Down the road, she was thinking about graduate school, perhaps a PhD or medical degree—or both.

Cycling alone offers sparse career opportunities for women. There are fewer teams, fewer big races, and fewer riders. USA Cycling's membership is roughly 87 percent male. In the United States, women's races generally have much smaller fields than the men's races. At Marian, a top male racer may be racing against seventy others in the "A," or most advanced, collegiate races. A women's field that same day may have just twenty contestants. And because of those smaller fields, some women quickly can advance to the upper categories of

Sinead Miller enjoys her Philly success. Photo by Daniel Lee

racing, meaning that crashes can be caused by less experienced bike handlers sharing the pack with seasoned racers.

Women also face issues of gender identity in sports that male athletes do not, according to Kristin Keim, a Category 1 racer and doctoral student in clinical psychology at John F. Kennedy University in California. Even top female racers, she said, face people who are surprised to learn that there even are teams for women pro racers. When many people picture an athlete in their minds, they think of a male, aggressive and strong. Keim recalled once riding her bike up a long climb. Some men were chasing her from behind, failing to make up ground on her. When they finally got near her, they remarked, "We thought you were a dude." It was a comment she didn't appreciate. Yet Keim said she tried to maintain her identity as a woman while racing. She didn't mind a compliment on her diamond earrings by the man holding her bike at the start of a big time trial.

Of course, both women and men experience many of the same ups and downs while developing as riders: the adjustment to Europe's tougher racing, the devastating crashes, the thrill of winning and being part of a cohesive team. "We do the same things the men do," Olds said. "We just don't get the media attention."

There is also, perhaps, another cultural phenomenon at work in women's cycling. It's difficult to look at women's cycling without being impressed by many of the riders' academic and career accomplishments. Since it's tough to make a living on the bike, they often have impressive credentials off the bike.

Some see it as part of a multitasking culture. "For the women's peloton, being a professional cyclist is part of a pattern of being an overachiever in general," said Dr. Dawn Richardson, who herself has at various times juggled titles of mom, racer, ER doc, and cycling team physician. Many men skip college or drop out of college to pursue pro cycling. But Richardson said with less money and recognition available to women, many female riders are driven by an urge to be overachievers. "It seems like it is just about a requirement for female cyclists to have a PhD or master's degree in something." Many women's racers come to cycling as young adults after competing in other sports.

Evelyn Stevens, a former tennis player for Dartmouth College, was the subject of a 2009 *Wall Street Journal* profile on her transition from a twenty-something Wall Street investment professional to an elite cyclist. Stevens first tried bike racing by entering a cycle-cross race in Northern California in 2007. In 2010, she rode for the prestigious HTC-Columbia women's team. The *Journal* article noted other quick ascents by women who previously had been focused on other sports or careers: Christine Thorburn, a physician, is a two-

Peanut Butter & Co. Twenty12 rode at the front of the pack throughout the day in Philadelphia. Photo by Darrell Parks, darrellparks.com

time Olympian. Abbott—the rider Miller helped win the Giro Donne—transitioned from being a swimmer at Washington State's Whitman College to a star of women's cycling.

The *Journal*'s story on Stevens ran under the bold headline CYCLING'S ONE-IN-A-MILLION STORY. The article stated that in women's cycling the talent was not as deep as in men's, allowing women with natural ability to, at times, stand out without much training. As the article aptly pointed out, though, long-term international success does not necessarily follow a quick rise into the ranks of the elite.

Miller already had proved she had the potential to have a long and fruitful career in racing. And unlike many women, she had started racing BMX at age five and road bikes at ten. She grew up on two wheels.

By 2010, she had improved from primarily a sprint specialist to a sleek all-around rider. Her personal coach, USA Cycling's Benjamin Sharp, saw an almost boundless potential in Miller. "She's always amazing me, so I really don't know what her limits are because I don't think we've even come close to them," he said. "She's always able to push." Teammate Olds put it more bluntly: "She is a champion."

But as the 2010 season neared its end, Miller faced a much different reality. A horrific crash in Holland left her unconscious for several minutes. She remembered nothing of the accident, which left her with a serious head injury, lost teeth, and facial fractures.

Miller had been racing for a chance to compete in the world championships. In an instant she faced a long recovery and an uncertain future in cycling. Her parents had purchased travel-medical insurance to transport her home in case of such an accident. Her head pounded on the transatlantic flight. She was missing teeth and beaten up. "All of the people were looking at me like I was crazy," Miller remembered.

She was a disturbing sight for her parents, who had built much of their own lives around supporting and nurturing their daughter's racing. "I think she came close to dying. I don't think she was far away from that," said Rex Miller, her father. "When she came home and I looked at her and saw her . . . I said, 'You have to be careful what you wish for.'"

Back home in South Park, near Pittsburgh, Miller would begin her recovery. She suffered bouts of depression. Her first cognitive tests were not good. She was hardly able to get out of bed for more than a month. She would sit out a semester at Marian University to recover. By October, she was feeling better though still suffering the effects of her head injury. Disturbingly, it was her third concussion in only about a year of racing.

"I'm definitely a little slow, still foggy at times. But I'll make it work. I'll make it happen," Miller said in October. "It was really tough at first, to be honest. I was not in good shape at first. The doctors were blunt with me. They were definitely very, very worried. I started to do a ton of rehab. I don't even know if they thought I was going to be better, like 100 percent again. But I have recovered so quickly, and I have to thank the Lord for that because it has been like a miracle."

Indeed, that month she started to feel better and started going on rides over hilly western Pennsylvania terrain. On the autumn day I talked with her, Miller had completed a four-hour ride. She talked excitedly about an international calendar of racing in 2011 with the newly formed Diadora-Pasta Zara-Manhattan women's professional cycling team, where her teammates would include Olds and Abbott.

Sharp, her coach, said the repeat concussions had become the biggest limiter for Miller. But he wasn't thinking much about her racing: "My number one concern for her is her overall health. Yeah, she did a four-hour ride, but that wasn't my prescription," he said. "I'm much more concerned how she's functioning in the next five or ten years than whether she's winning bike races in the next five or ten years."

Sharp discussed how he communicated with younger athletes over contentious issues such as coming back from injury. At times, he has to draw on the athlete's emotions and lay out a worst-case scenario. Miller, he said, is very driven and stubborn. He had to be stern with her.

"When you're nineteen years old, a year is forever, but when you're looking at a career that could span ten or fifteen years, taking a year off to address an injury is inconsequential," Sharp said. "So you just have to help, especially, younger athletes keep perspective and understand that there's a day after tomorrow."

Sharp assembled a sort of care team for Miller and organized a conference call among himself, her doctor, her parents, Marian University cycling coach Dean Peterson, and an expert on head injuries from the US Olympic Committee.

After several months of rehab in Pennsylvania, Miller was set to return to Marian University in Indianapolis for the winter 2011 semester. She would take a full course load and again get used to the demands of being a college student. "She's got everything she ever wanted yet she has this thing, this big hurdle to get over," Peterson said of her injury. "And she's in a place where I know she understands. I don't even think about having her on the team right now, I just want her to be okay."

Miller had created a situation where she could pursue her academic and cycling dreams simultaneously at Marian. Starting as a freshman in 2008, Miller had balanced regular trips to Europe with the US National Team with her studies. She was an A student majoring in chemistry and math. She was on a cycling scholarship that covered her tuition and fees, $24,960 for the 2010–2011 academic year. She'd keep in touch with professors over the Internet as she traveled the world racing bikes.

Marian, with an enrollment of about twenty-three hundred, was one of a small handful of schools where she could find that sort of opportunity.

The university's campus sits next to Indianapolis's Major Taylor Velodrome, the banked cycling track that has hosted many championships and competitions including the 1987 Pan American Games. Years later, school officials sought to use the banked track and the growing popularity of collegiate cycling as a way to attract cyclists to their campus and showcase their small school. Marian and other small institutions such as Lees-McRae College in North Carolina and Fort Lewis College in Colorado are among a niche of colleges and universities to treat cycling in the same way as traditional college sports. These teams have coaches and provide financial support for top riders. At most universities, even those with strong bike-racing traditions, cycling remains a club sport.

Dean Peterson, a longtime teacher and bicycle racer, was hired by Marian to be an instructor in the school of education as well as the cycling coach. In trying to build up Marian's cycling team, Peterson focused much of his attention on boosting the women's squad.

Gender equity is a hot topic across collegiate athletics. Yet collegiate cycling—which is sanctioned by USA Cycling, not the NCAA—simplifies this contentious area by scoring men's and women's results together when it comes to crowning national champions. Coed combined scoring is the equalizer—even a great men's team likely won't win a national title without some help from the women.

A male or female can become an individual champion in the road race or criterium, or win the individual omnium in collegiate cycling. But the team champion is determined by the combined scores of each school's men and women, with each gender counting equally.

"It truly made me actually recruit the women's angle first," Peterson said.

In 2008, Miller became his prize catch. But she took some work to land. He had long scouted her race results. He called her Pittsburgh-area home and left repeated phone messages. Miller, though, already had made plans to attend Penn State University to major in chemical engineering. Yet Peterson persisted with the calls, and eventually talked Miller into visiting Marian.

Peterson sat with Miller and her father, Rex, and touted Marian's math and science programs, the school's cycling team, and the support and flexibility the small school could provide to her as a student and athlete. Marian would work to accommodate her when her racing schedule took her from the classroom.

As Miller went off to visit with some of the female riders at Marian, Peterson talked with Rex. Miller's father, a former motorcycle racer, showed Peterson the van they had traveled from Pennsylvania in: a fully decked-out cycling-support vehicle. In the cargo area was a shop with fork mounts for bikes and a motorcycle for motor-paced training.

As he visited with Miller and her father, Peterson knew he was on the brink of getting his top recruit: an elite rider who also was a serious student with, on top of all that, a radiant personality. He even wondered if he, as a coach, was ready to help advance such a driven talent. "This is the diamond . . . it's not even in the rough," Peterson thought as he talked with Miller. He hoped she'd pick Marian. He hoped he was ready to coach a rider of her talent and potential.

Miller had come into road racing through the intense and physical world of BMX racing. Around four years old, she told her parents that BMX racing looked like fun as the family drove by the local track on the way home from church. Soon she was riding and racing at the South Park BMX track near Pittsburgh. The Millers had lived in nearby Brentwood, but when Miller was about ten they moved to a house within easy biking distance of the track. Miller excelled, so much so that she looked for more competition against the larger fields of male riders.

When the rules prevented Miller from competing against boys, she would tuck her long hair into her helmet and race anyway. Eventually, her mom threatened legal action to clear the way for her to race against male riders. Miller was competing in sixty or seventy races a year—her racing schedule dominated the family's weekends for nine months a year. She developed toughness on the dirt track. "It's almost like throwing a girl out on a football field," Rex said. "It's not a timid sport. She'd get her elbows out . . . She was very aggressive, a really, really gutsy rider." Miller's father remembered after their visit to the Indianapolis campus driving home to Pennsylvania with his daughter initially telling him she didn't want to attend Marian. They got home and talked more. Penn State offered big-time college life with strong academics and the lure of Nittany Lion football games. Marian offered a small-college education with a dedicated cycling program and flexibility from professors to balance her course work with her racing schedule.

Miller, her father said, simply woke up one morning and said she had decided to attend Marian. Once on campus, she made a quick impact. As a freshman in 2009, Miller overcame a nasty case of bronchitis to win the collegiate criterium national championship. At five-foot-eight and then weighing up to 160 pounds, Miller was well built for the aggressive positioning and sprinting required to win criteriums.

Yet she aimed for international success. "I really, really wanted to do well over in Europe. That's my goal. I want to win the world championships one day," Miller said. "I want to be an Olympic champion, and you're not going to do that unless you're really fit and can climb. I didn't want to be just a crit rider."

So from September 2009 through January 2010, she changed her diet. She cut out most meats except for lean cuts such as turkey. She ate lots of vegetables. She would eat oatmeal, but not the higher-fat granola. She lost close to forty pounds. Miller transformed herself from looking like a solid basketball player into looking more like a sleek runner. Peterson worried she had lost the weight too quickly. Yet she was riding faster than ever.

She finished third in the road race and fifth in the criterium in the Division I collegiate cycling championship in May at Madison, Wisconsin. On the third and final day of the competition, Miller helped lead Marian's four-woman squad to a victory in the team time trial. Together with a strong showing by the men's team, Marian captured the overall team omnium title. Throughout the season, she'd confirm her standing as one of the nation's top young female cyclists— a legitimate 2012 Olympic hopeful.

Professional male cyclists have the Tour de France and famous one-day races such as Paris–Roubaix from which to build careers and gain fame. For women, without events commanding global media coverage, events such as the Olympics and world championships tend to become their best shots at glory.

Miller's friend and teammate Shelley Olds said her ultimate goal was to represent the United States in the 2012 Olympic road race in London—although Olds, born in 1980, added that she hopes to race for many years after that. Unlike Miller, Olds was a latecomer to cycling. She grew up in Massachusetts playing soccer. She attended Roanoke College in Virginia, where she earned a degree in health and human performance and was captain of the women's soccer team. After graduation, she moved to Gilroy in Northern California. "I didn't have a soccer team to play for, but I still had my competitive edge and need for sport," said Olds. Cycling, a popular activity in the Bay Area, was a natural fit. Soon after starting to ride, she was competing in just about every form of bike racing—road, track cyclo-cross, tandems, and mountain bikes. She blossomed on the track, but after changes by cycling's international governing body eliminated her event from the Olympic velodrome program, she switched her focus solely to road racing.

And just as many up-and-coming American male cyclists see big differences between US and European racing, so does Olds. She found European racing to be faster, more tactical. She also saw differences in how countries develop promising young riders. The United States, Olds said, is a big country with loads of potential cycling talent. Many of its talented female cyclists start the sport in their twenties, not as teenagers. It can be a shock once those women get their first taste of international racing.

"It sort of becomes a crash-and-burn or succeed-and-thrive phenomenon," Olds said. "And because we are such a big country with so much talent to be identified, there is little concern for the ones that crash and burn. The contrast is in the smaller European countries, where there is not an abundance of talent or riders to choose from. The federation must first identify talent and interest in women, and then develop it from a young age. So you see women racing from a very young age, and you see the progression year after year."

In many ways, Miller is an example of an American rider nurtured from a young age; an athlete who progressed year after year. Olds and Miller represent the two ends of women's cycling—one the gutsy little girl who loved BMX, the other the fit twenty-something professional woman looking for a competitive outlet.

Olds, as the 2011 season was set to begin, said she was honored to have Miller as a teammate. "We will have fun, I am sure," she said.

Yet Miller still faced her ongoing recovery from her head injury. Her father, Rex, the former motorcycle racer, realized that such risks are part of high-speed sports. "She's one crash from never racing again. She's got to finish her education." He knew she loved school and excelled in it. Yet he also knew his daughter's passion for cycling. She got up at 5 AM to train. She trained in weather so cold her water bottle froze.

The proud and concerned dad said, "She's definitely the whole package."

Ripping Their Hearts Out

My alarm awoke me at 3:45 AM for my long drive that day from my home near Indianapolis to Greenville, South Carolina, for the USA Cycling Professional Championships. Soon I drove out of my dark and empty neighborhood and headed south.

It was mid-September 2010. Summer was blending into autumn, yet even at this early hour it was still warm enough to be comfortable in shorts and a short-sleeved shirt. It would be a hot and sunny weekend in South Carolina. The 2010 cycling season—and my journey to discover what it takes for young Americans to become professionals—neared its climax. The winners of Saturday's 20.7-mile time trial and Sunday's 115-mile road race each would earn a national champion's stars-and-stripes jersey. US cycling mainstays George Hincapie and Levi Leipheimer were among those competing, as were some of the young riders I had been with in Belgium in the spring, namely Taylor Phinney, Benjamin King, and Daniel Holloway.

American cycling had developed over the decades to the point that races could have multiple story lines and rivalries. This year, much of the attention was on US cycling's new and old guard: Could Phinney challenge Leipheimer for the time trial title? Could Hincapie defend his road-race title in his hometown?

I thought about such things as I drove past the rolling horse farms of Lexington, Kentucky, with the early-morning mist lingering over the pastures. The evolution of the US professional championship itself was another sign of just how far the sport had come since I first watched Greg LeMond on television in the mid-1980s. The United States has always been something of a quirky outsider in this tradition-bound Western European sport. Nations such as France, Belgium, and Italy all crowned their professional national time trial and road-race champions in June—the timing allowed the winners to show off their championship jerseys in the Tour de France and throughout the summer racing season.

From 1985 through 2005, the US professional champion was decided in June in Philadelphia. But the race—which has changed its name over the years along with its sponsor—also included international riders. The logic in the beginning was that because the United States had so few professional cyclists, riders and teams from other nations were needed to fill out a top field. Olympic speed skating legend Eric Heiden, then racing for 7-Eleven, won the race in 1985, providing needed star power for the new event. In 1993, then-twenty-one-year-old Lance Armstrong of Team Motorola pumped his fists in victory down the finishing stretch to claim a solo victory. But other years, the US pro championship was a confusing race within a race. A successful breakaway or sprint by foreign-born riders would leave the US cyclists trying not necessarily to win, but to be the first American to cross the line—that was good enough to win the national championship.

In 2006, USA Cycling moved the professional road-race championship from Philadelphia to Greenville, making it an event open only to US citizens. An individual time trial championship also was added. What's more, the Greenville races would be held in September, not June.

The first four races in Greenville were dominated by American cycling's heavyweights. Hincapie, who lives in Greenville, won in 2006 and 2009. Fellow veteran Leipheimer took the title in 2007 and Tyler Hamilton, who had returned from a doping ban (he soon would retire after another failed test), placed first in 2008. David Zabriskie had captured the time trial championship from 2006 through 2009 but would not be defending his title because he was in Europe. (In 2011, USA Cycling moved the pro championships from September to Memorial Day weekend, to put itself closer in line with other nations.)

Now, not too many things are worth getting up at 3:45 AM for. But I wanted to make sure I arrived in Greenville in time for a 3 PM news conference—Taylor Phinney was one of the featured riders. I had not seen Phinney since his dramatic stage win in Belgium's Triptyque des Monts et Châteaux five months before. His season had been filled with impressive wins—including his second straight victory at the under-twenty-three Paris–Roubaix and stage wins in America at the Tour of Gila and Tour of Utah—as well as some high-speed crashes. As he walked into the Friday-afternoon press conference wearing shorts and a MELLOW JOHNNY'S bike shop T-shirt, his arm and leg still carried the scabs from his crash days before in the Tour de l'Avenir in France. "That's just cycling," Phinney told me before the press conference. "You have ups and downs constantly. For me, I've had really high ups and not-too-low downs. Yeah, it's been good."

Phinney was looking for another high note in Greenville. In the days before the US Pro Championships, Phinney had been a guest in George Hincapie's new villa-style home set high atop a hill overlooking Greenville. Hincapie's home—with its edgeless pool in the backyard and large portrait of his wife, Melanie, a former Tour de France podium model, in the living room—was a tangible sign of the veteran rider's long and successful career. "We have similar traits," said Hincapie, after I asked him whether Phinney reminded him of himself at that age. "He's probably been more successful than I was at this point." Soon after the Greenville weekend, Phinney would confirm that he'd be racing for Hincapie's BMC Racing Team.

A professional national time trial championship at the age of twenty would go far in reaffirming Phinney as America's new cycling star. Saturday's 20.7-mile national championship time trial consisted of three 6.9-mile laps of a slightly rolling and windy course around the Clemson University International Center for Automotive Research and surrounding Greenville suburban streets. The time trial, which had just fifteen entrants, was expected to come down to one marquee matchup: Phinney versus Leipheimer, the twenty-year-old phenom versus the thirty-six-year-old veteran.

As I sat in the front row waiting for Friday's news conference—a bit tired from my nine-hour drive—I anticipated some lively lines from the always quotable Phinney. He didn't disappoint. "I've beaten Levi before, but he was not wearing a skinsuit," he said, referring to his two-second victory a month before in the Tour of Utah, when in fact Leipheimer was not wearing his aerodynamic Team Radio Shack skinsuit. Phinney wanted a totally even contest.

Then Phinney let loose a particularly memorable line: "I'm just going to go out there and rip my heart out for you guys," he told the crowd. His one-liner would turn out to be the theme for the weekend of racing in Greenville.

Road racing—with its speed, tactics, and the whoosh of the peloton—is the most alluring of cycling events. But there's something almost sacred about the time trial: Each rider left alone on the course to suffer. I thought about that as I stood near the start house. Each rider took his turn sitting in a tense silence for those final moments before rolling down the ramp at the start line. Some placed ice stuffed into small bags made of pantyhose down their backs to cool themselves from the warm Southern sun. Some stretched nervously or shook beefy quadriceps to stay loose. Phinney and Leipheimer—strikingly different in size, at six-foot-four and five-foot-seven, respectively—were the final two riders to start. The two men sat next to each other in the start house in those final moments before their duel. All was quiet until Leipheimer looked over at Phinney and, with a wide smile, said: "Tear your heart out." Leipheimer raised his clinched hand up for a fist bump with Phinney. It was a private show of sportsmanship from the older rider.

Phinney completed the first of the three 6.9-mile laps in 13:26, which put him about 15 seconds faster than Leipheimer. By the end of the second lap, Leipheimer had cut Phinney's lead to eight seconds. Leipheimer held his tiny aero tuck, his face just about touching his hands as he clasped the ends of his handlebars. With no race radios to get time-split information, the two had to simply gun it until the finish without knowing exactly how far they were apart. Yet Leipheimer had envisioned just such a scenario: him taking back precious seconds from Phinney in the race's closing miles. "He's world pursuit champ. He's used to starting fast. He's got younger legs," Leipheimer said. "My advantage is the length. The efficiency. The experience. Pacing. Those are the things that are on my side. I just tried to focus on the last lap."

Phinney's race strategy was the opposite: He hit the first lap hard, maybe too hard, he admitted afterward. He suffered for that effort on the last two laps, but he knew how to ride the course, pushing through on the uphill portions and using his long legs and size to gain time on the flat and downhill portions. Phinney crossed the finish line with a time of 41:02:51. He quickly turned his bike around and pedaled back to the finish area to await the arrival of Leipheimer. After 3 long minutes, Leipheimer came into view . . . the clock whirling his time too quickly for the human mind to compute the margin between the two men . . . 40:59 . . . 41:00 . . . 41:01 . . .

The digital numbers on the clock affixed atop the finishing banner stopped whirling at 41:02:65—Phinney had won the national time trial championship by 0.14 second—fourteen one-hundredths of a second. Jelly Belly's Bernard Van Ulden, with a time of 42:15, was a distant third.

Phinney rolled back across the finish line, raising his arm in celebration and wiping his brow in relief after seeing his razor-thin margin of victory. On the podium, he squeezed his frame into what appeared to be a size small US champion's jersey and joked, "This is Levi's size."

Leipheimer, though clearly disappointed, made no excuses. "You could count a hundred places where I lost 0.14 of a second. But anybody could do that. Taylor can do that . . . It just takes some time to get over the disappointment. Sometimes it's good to have a stinging defeat like that. Sometimes you need that to kick it in gear, to re-

Taylor Phinney squeezes into a tight-fitting champion's jersey.
Levi Leipheimer is left dejected.
Photo by Darrell Parks, darrellparks.com

motivate yourself. I guess I'm just looking on the bright side."

Phinney already was enjoying another moment in the spotlight. On the victory podium and at the post-race news conference, he sported Oakley Eyeshades—a version of the oversized 1980s-era sports sunglasses worn by his father, Davis, and 7-Eleven teammate Andy Hampsten a generation ago. A reporter asked him what was with the unusual shades resting atop his forehead. "My dad used to wear these. He used to look pretty good in them," Phinney said, before adding drily: "But I think that was the whole '80s thing. I can't really pull it off because we live in a modern society." Upon request, he then pulled the shades down from his forehead over his eyes—in fact over almost half his face—and mugged for the cameras, his championship medal dangling from around his neck, as he held his crystal-glass winner's trophy.

He wore a grin as wide as his retro shades.

Cycling remains a marginalized sport in the United States, with most mainstream media mentions about either Lance Armstrong or doping. Yet in a midsized city like Greenville, the USA Cycling Pro Championships was big enough that its influence could be seen throughout town. I rode in the BMC Racing Team car with the team's media man, Sean Weide, who remarked on how many people were staring into the car—most likely looking for hometown rider Hincapie. I headed to Chipotle my first night in Greenville for a burrito only to see guys from the UnitedHealthcare Pro Cycling Team also there to carbo-load. The next morning, Saturday, with fuel left over from my burrito, I headed to Altamont Road to ride over Paris Mountain—the major climb for Sunday's 115-mile championship road race. I parked my car at a nearby CVS drugstore, unloaded my Bianchi racing bike, and started pedaling up the long hill, going the opposite direction the riders would be racing. Ahead of me, a truck and crew were descending the hill to set up straw bales along the edge of the course to protect riders in case of high-speed crashes. They set bales against trees, mailboxes, road signs, and along the tightest turns in the roadway. I crested the top of the hill and descended to the bottom of the other side for the opportunity to ride the same direction as the riders the next day. Dozens of other recreational cyclists were out on the hill doing the same thing—testing their legs on the same course the pros would be riding.

As I turned around and began to climb again, I tried to keep my speed around nine or ten miles per hour on the climb. But I did receive some nice encouragement partway up when two attractive women in a car with Georgia plates pulled alongside and the driver yelled, "Nice job!" I enjoyed the pain and strain of climbing as I crested the hill and began the descent the riders would navigate four times in Sunday's race. As I leaned into corners and whizzed past pine trees, I thought about what the race would be like: first the sound of shifting as chains skipped from climbing gears to descending gears, and then the whooshing sound of carbon fiber cutting through the wind. The riders, drenched in sweat and anaerobic from the climb, then would begin the highly technical task of descending. The rider goes from sitting straight in the saddle or standing for high-resistance pedal strokes to a crunched high-speed aero tuck. One moment sweat pours down the rider's face and body at slow speed; the next, perspiration streams uncontrollably into his eyes or is ripped from his body by high-speed wind resistance. It's a switch in mentality more abrupt than a wide receiver who, in an instant, goes from trying to catch a pass to trying to tackle a defender after an interception.

On Sunday morning, I arrived at the start–finish area in downtown Greenville more than two hours ahead of the road race's scheduled 1 PM start time. This would be another warm, sunny day—ninety degrees and blue skies. I ventured to the parking lot, where the team vans pulled in with bikes crowded on roof racks. Each van was an anthill of activity: Soigneurs prepared food and water bottles, mechanics examined bikes, riders got out of vehicles and walked and stretched like someone who had just exited a car after a long trip. Riders tooled about on bikes or simply sat in foldable cloth chairs—

pro riders love sitting wherever and whenever possible to save any energy they'll need later. I spotted Daniel Holloway by the Team Bissell van. He sat loading food and energy gels into small containers. We chatted for a bit; Holloway was friendly but preoccupied with the day ahead. I patted him on the back and headed back to the start line.

The crowd there began to grow. Two young women with long blond hair, shorts, and sandals eyed riders signing in for the race. A small but enthusiastic cheer followed hometown rider Hincapie down the road as he pedaled toward the start line. The 1 PM race time approached. First, the riders of note were called to the line, Levi Leipheimer, Taylor Phinney, and George Hincapie among them. Then the rest of the field of roughly eighty riders rolled forward. Daniel Holloway of Team Bissell squeezed into the front row, right next to Phinney. After a solo trumpeter's rendition of "The Star-Spangled Banner," the riders were off—first, for three laps of a 4-mile circuit around Greenville, then four roughly 22-mile loops that each included the 2.2-mile Paris Mountain climb, and then three more circuits of the 4-mile loop to finish. An estimated eighty thousand would watch the race.

Benjamin King, riding for the Trek-Livestrong team, rolled off the front of the pack in the race's opening mile. The twenty-one-year-old King, almost without trying, had a small gap. "Go, dude!" yelled teammate Phinney, more joking around than serious. Yet King did go. Holloway—who had ridden with King in Europe as part of the US National Development Team—sprinted up to King, as did Scott Zwizanski of the Kelly Benefits Strategy Team. The breakaway immediately began gaining time on the pack . . . one minute, two minutes. This was a good combination: King loved long breakaways, having won junior and under-twenty-three national championships with solo attacks. Holloway was under team orders to try to get in any early move. And Holloway also had a knack for playing to the crowd, making dramatic moves. Zwizanski—or Zwiz as he's known—was a time trial specialist able to drive the pace into the wind. The early pace was fast enough that a rider from Team Mountain Khakis was left behind quickly by the breakaway.

The pack spread itself across the roadway at an almost leisurely pace. Early breakaways rarely survive, and the peloton collectively knew that.

Up front, King and Holloway traded a joke about what Jim Miller—the USA Cycling honcho who coached the two riders—would make of their early attack. Miller had told both to be patient, to save their energy for the finish. Indeed, King worried he was throwing away his chances; he envisioned being baked alive under the hot Southern sun—he'd be crispy roadkill by the time the pack overcame him and his two breakaway companions. Yet he, Zwizanski, and Holloway were committed. They rode team-time-trial-style, each taking turns at the front—the rider cutting into the wind often would rest his forearms atop his handlebars, his hands dangling over the front wheel, in an effort to get in a more aerodynamic position. Behind, the peloton was unmotivated. Team Radio Shack, led by veterans Leipheimer and Chris Horner, was not about to chase down King, who rode for Trek-Livestrong—a team sponsored by Radio Shack and owned by Shack rider Lance Armstrong. "When one big strong team isn't motivated to chase, it really demotivates the field. Other teams, even if they do help, it's not 100 percent," said Kiel Reijnen, of Team Jelly Belly, after the race.

The lead ballooned from five minutes to ten minutes before reaching an eventual peak of more than seventeen minutes. Holloway was relieved by the large lead. Now the group could ride the Paris Mountain climb at a moderate pace, and pedal harder on the flat and rolling portions of the course to maintain its lead. King set the tempo at the front the first time up Paris Mountain. On the second ascent, Holloway set the pace at the bottom with King taking over for the second half. King wasn't satisfied with a moderate pace. "Zwiz and I had to tell him to take it down a notch, that we didn't have to ride that hard on this part of the climb," Holloway said afterward. "He looked a little frustrated. Obviously, he was going so well."

Daniel Holloway in the early break on a hot South Carolina day.
Photo by Darrell Parks, darrellparks.com

The third of the total four times up Paris Mountain, King kept riding his tempo, which was fast enough to leave behind Holloway and
Zwizanski—this was decision time. King later said he felt guilty for
violating the unspoken code for early-race breakaways: Stick together
as long as possible. Yet he also hated seeing his lead shrink to twelve
minutes. Holloway and Zwizanski decided that they would stick together. "He's either going to wait for us, or he's going to ride away,"
Holloway said.

King rode away.

He began to feel the crowd sensing that he could win. Drawing energy from the fans, King jokingly took a beer handout from partying
fans on Paris Mountain.* The next time up, the fans had a keg wait-

*Benjamin King, besides being an aspiring professional cyclist, is an aspiring writer.
This chapter includes pieces of his written description of his race. It is a true lens into
his thoughts that day.

ing for him—King ignored that. After the third time up Paris Mountain, King's lead was nine minutes. The race was simple now: stay away and win, or get caught and have no hope of a high placing. King's head whirled with thoughts: His father, Mark, and sister Hannah were along the course watching him. *Keep going for them.* He prayed. *God must have something to do with the situation I'm in,* King thought.

Salt from evaporated sweat crusted on his Trek-Livestrong shorts, turning the black Lycra partially white. Holloway and Zwizanski—midway between King and the pack—had no chance of winning. As they passed through the start–finish area, Holloway waved his arm up and down, egging the crowd on to cheer for their effort. Neither would finish the race.

King held a lead of 6:25 after the fourth and final climb of Paris Mountain. Was it enough? He was no longer capable of such calculations. His legs cramped. Yet behind him the chase was disorganized, King's rivals frustrated. "We're chasing but the gap's not coming down!" the BMC Racing Team's exasperated Assistant Director Michael Sayers yelled as he drove the team car behind the pack.

Three more laps of the finishing four-mile circuit remained: half an hour more in the fire. King's vision blurred. He noticed weird things: bulging veins in the necks of screaming fans. He worried he was so depleted he could lose consciousness. The Team Radio Shack car pulled alongside King. "You deserve this!" yelled Allen Lim, the team's exercise physiologist. "This is for the jersey! It's yours! You're making history! This is history!"

The end was near—the finish line in sight. He had made it. King zipped up his jersey and raised his arms in victory. Holloway, who had dropped out of the race after being caught by the pack, waited just past the finish line with a big smile as King rode by in victory. Holloway simply smiled and applauded. King came to a stop. Holloway hugged him. Then King was quickly surrounded by photographers as he fell to the ground in exhaustion. More than a minute and a half

Benjamin King knew he'd never give up but feared losing
consciousness in the agonizing final miles.
Photo by Darrell Parks, darrellparks.com

passed before Alex Candelario of the Kelly Benefit Strategies team
sprinted in for second and Reijnen of Jelly Belly for third.

And so the US professional cycling road race championship would
end with a surprise champion, crumpled to the pavement in a joyous depletion. He looked as if he could cry from happiness, or per-

haps puke from his effort. He stood up and with reporters' recorders and microphones outstretched, searched for words. "I thought, I'm throwing my race away," he said of his early attack. He talked about his legs cramping and his mind praying.

Teammate Phinney—who had just finished eighth in the final sprint—charged over and bear-hugged King. "Holy shit!" Phinney yelled. Then came King's father, Mark. Crying from a release of joy and amazement, Dad wrapped his arms around his son. "Your mother has been praying for you all race," he said. King, tight in the embrace, closed his eyes and smiled.

I stood at a respectful distance and watched. Part of a reporter's job is to be a voyeur during such personal moments—it's an often awkward and detached job. Yet I was emotionally involved. I had been in Belgium with Phinney, King, and Holloway that spring, when in one race King's knee had been ripped up by another rider's chainring in a crash. I knew he had ridden eighty-six miles with a shredded leg that day. I knew King made the decision to leave Virginia Tech to pursue cycling full-time. I knew he read C. S. Lewis—who also was one of my favorite authors—to keep his faith fresh. I choked up and tears briefly flowed under my sunglasses and down my cheeks.

Yet I went about the reporter's task of gathering quotes in the race's aftermath. As King was taken away for doping tests and to prepare for the podium celebration, I tracked down his father, Mark: "He doesn't have the natural ability of Taylor Phinney, but he's got a work ethic and the heart of a lion . . . I'm turning fifty this year, so it's a great fiftieth birthday present!"

I found Phinney in the roadway in front of the stage where King soon would receive his national championship jersey and medal. I remarked to Phinney that three young riders now held the three major US pro road cycling titles: Holloway in the criterium, Phinney the time trial, and King the road race. King, at twenty-one, was now the youngest-ever winner of the US pro road title—months ahead of the then-twenty-one-year-old Lance Armstrong's 1993 title in

For Benjamin King, a sweet victory. For the determined
Kiel Reijnen, background left, an impressive third place.
Photo by Darrell Parks, darrellparks.com

Philadelphia. Phinney listened and responded: "Hey, man. I don't
know. It just goes to show we got the motors. With the right development, with the right mentorship, you can achieve what we've done
this weekend."

Just before Greenville, King and Phinney were in Europe racing
the Tour de l'Avenir stage race—a top race for young riders that trans-
lates to "tour of the future"—helping fellow American Andrew Talansky ride to a second place overall. King credited the gruntwork he
performed in that race with giving him the form he needed to win
in Greenville. King's hard lessons from European racing already were
paying off.

I stayed up until three o'clock the next morning in my Greenville
Days Inn room writing down my thoughts about the race and filing
my report for PezCyclingNews.com. After a short night's sleep, I
awoke at 8 AM, dressed, and walked through the lobby and outside

to a gas station just down the road to get a newspaper. I picked up a fresh copy of *The Greenville News* and paid my 75 cents. I unfolded the paper to see a photo of King—a surprised smile of joy crossing his face—being simultaneously kissed on each cheek by two podium girls. The headline read, YOUTH HAS ITS DAY IN PRO CYCLING RACE.

Out of the Vortex

The final months of 2010 brought the usual slew of end-of-season roster changes. Taylor Phinney moved from Trek-Livestrong to the BMC Racing Team. Benjamin King joined Team Radio Shack from Trek-Livestrong. Lawson Craddock left the Hot Tubes team to become part of Trek-Livestrong. Daniel Holloway moved from Bissell Pro Cycling to Kelly Benefits Pro Cycling. Kiel Reijnen left Jelly Belly for Team Type 1. And so on.

It's a natural cycle of professional cycling. Riders change. Teams change. The sport moves on with different players in different roles. But for some—including Guy East, twenty-three, of Indianapolis, and Jackson Stewart, thirty, of San Jose—2010 brought an end to their careers as professional cyclists. For East, it could just be a temporary break. For Stewart, it looked more like a career change.

East helped inspire me to write this book. He came out of the MOB Squad cycling team run by my longtime friend Mario Camacho. East advanced from local races in Indiana to ride for the US National Development Team in Belgium, for Trek-Livestrong, and for Kelly Benefits Strategies. He also specialized in six-day races on the velodrome. He was one of the first people I told about my book idea. He was the first rider I interviewed. Right away I could tell he was proud to be included in my project. His career was just beginning.

In late 2009, we met at a coffee shop in suburban Indianapolis. East told me of his goals in professional cycling, especially about wanting to compete in Europe's fall and winter circuit of professional six-day velodrome races.

"Sixes," as they're called, are tough to describe—even to cycling fans. Even Ernest Hemingway had a tough time putting these high-speed spectacles into words. Hemingway, in *A Moveable Feast,* wrote that he had started many stories on these races but had never written one as good as the competitions themselves. He was a regular at Six Days in Paris around the 1920s and concluded that French was the only language in which the races had ever been written about properly.

"It's mysterious," East said of Sixes. "It's almost romantic . . . No one understands it."

In modern-day Sixes, riders compete from roughly 6 PM to 2 AM for, well, six straight nights in indoor cycling tracks in cities such as Ghent, Zurich, Berlin, and Grenoble that more closely resemble beer halls or discotheques than sports arenas.

At the 2009 Grenoble Six Jours, East competed in an atmosphere Hemingway likely would have appreciated. Sports anthems such as "Stand Up for the Champions" welcomed riders to the track. Acrobats performed. Topless cabaret showgirls danced.

But the main attraction, as it always has been, was the racing: East and the other riders whirled elbow-to-elbow around the highly banked wood track at speeds reaching forty miles an hour. East's long blond hair flowed from the wind created by his own speed.

East discovered six-day racing as part of USA Cycling's National Development Team. In modern-day Sixes, riders compete on two-man teams. Each night's racing comprises multiple events, including time trials and elimination races. But the marquee draw is the Madison.

In the Madison—named after New York's Madison Square Garden, where Six Days were popular a century ago—the two-rider teams take turns racing. When one rider is finishing his turn, he grabs hands with his teammate and slings him into the action.

Once, Sixes were a round-the-clock competition. But even racing from 6 PM to 2 AM takes its toll. East started the Grenoble race with a stomach bug that was causing him to vomit. Yet he felt stronger as the race progressed, winning an elimination race on day 5. East and

Guy East, left, clasps hands with partner Austin Carroll for a Madison sling during the 2009 Grenoble Six Day. Photo by Edmond Hood

Massage time for Guy East in rider's cabin at the Grenoble Six Day. Photo by Edmond Hood

partner Austin Carroll, who also fought a bug, finished tenth out of eleven teams overall. It was a starting point for newcomers to this hard man's form of racing.

East is easygoing and comes across as shy. Yet he also has a quiet, almost mischievous confidence. As a teenager attending the 2003 world championships in Canada, East encountered German sprint legend Erik Zabel—the six-time winner of the Tour de France's green points jersey—talking to reporters. He asked Zabel if he could have his cycling cap. No, the answer came back. East responded by snatching the cap from Zabel's head anyway and sprinting away. Years later, he returned the hat to the retiring Zabel at a six-day race. Zabel laughed as he took back his cap.

As we sat in that suburban coffee shop, East's eyes sparkled when he talked about six-day racing in a way they did not when he talked about road racing. It was, perhaps, a clue that East was not on the same trajectory as many of the other riders featured in this book.

Road racing—the Tour de France at the pinnacle—is where the money, fans, and fame are in cycling.

East had chased his cycling dreams full-on. After graduating from Heritage Christian High School in 2006, he did not enroll in college. East raced year-round: spring and summer on the road, and fall and winter on the track. In 2009, he estimated he had flown a hundred thousand miles to and from races.

Was this a path to burnout? Perhaps.

As I started working on this book, I sought to learn more about East. I also developed an admiration for him. It became apparent that this was a young man who possessed a passion for learning and people.

Edmond Hood, who writes for the cycling website PezCyclingNews.com, told me that East has what it takes to make it on the six-day circuit. Yet it was interesting that Hood pointed more to East's personality than to his raw cycling power.

"It's a life that requires self-sufficiency as well as athletic ability," Hood said of six-day racing. "It struck me that Guy has that quality." Hood added that East had a way of connecting with other riders, of making friends. In six-day racing, riders are not paid salaries but instead sign contracts for each six-day race—if a rider crashes out with a broken collarbone, he loses his pay. On the tight confines of the track, six-day riders who brashly and needlessly cause crashes are despised. "You need friends to make it far in Sixes," Hood said.

Early in reporting my book, I asked Noel Dejonckheere about East. His blunt answer revealed, perhaps, a clue of what was yet to come. East, Dejonckheere said, was "too easygoing for himself." He could be good in team time trials and at working hard at the front of the pack. He said East had ability but could lose his focus. Dejonckheere added, "Guy is a really nice guy. But sometimes he is just too nice."

East had things outside cycling on his mind. He was troubled by the poverty he had seen while racing in Mexico and the Philippines. He also saw the raw side of his sport.

In November 2009, East showed his father a photo from the Grenoble Six Day in which he had competed. He pointed to a rider in a photo, Belgian Dimitri De Fauw, and told his dad that De Fauw had apparently killed himself shortly after the race ended. According to media reports, De Fauw had been depressed after a crash in which he was involved at the 2006 Ghent Six Day killed Spanish cyclist Isaac Galvez. East's father, Guy Sr.—the man who guided and mentored his son into cycling—tried to remind his son of opportunities in life to reach out to people in need, to share with people their Christian beliefs. It's part of the faith that guided East into adulthood and continued to shape his worldview.

And so in November 2010—about a year after I sat with East in the coffee shop talking about six-day racing and his burgeoning career—we sat in a trendy pizza restaurant in the same suburban shopping plaza discussing his decision to take a break from bike racing.

East had just finished a season of road racing with the Kelly Benefits Pro Cycling Team. In September, I had seen him race in the US Professional Road Championship in Greenville, South Carolina. I saw him near the front of the pack early in the race, but then he disappeared. As his close friend Benjamin King won, East was among the many riders to not finish.

We ordered a couple Belgian-style beers, bread sticks, and two gourmet-style pizzas: one with four cheeses, the other with home-made sausage. He told me about being at a party with other riders after the US Professional Championships in Greenville in September. East had heard one top rider ask another, "Are you going to have a piece of pizza, or ride the world championships?" Such a question—perhaps a joke, partly indicative of the strictness of a rider's life—came on a day the two riders had just raced 115 miles.

Now East could enjoy his pizza. We each ordered a second beer. And for almost two hours, we talked. I noticed East was wearing a gray MELLOW JOHNNY'S T-shirt from Lance Armstrong's bike shop in Austin—he had worn the same shirt when we met for coffee a year before. Over pizza and beer we talked about God, about humanity, and about distant lands. And of course we talked about bikes. Our waiter, in his desire to be helpful, became a pest interrupting our conversation to check on us again and again. I wondered whether the middle-aged couple sitting next to us was eavesdropping. How could they not? Our conversation involved something rare in American society: a young man talking openly about his life.

East had weeks before had a similar conversation with Jonas Carney, the performance director of the Kelly Benefits team. Carney—a legendary sprinter on the US circuit who won four professional criterium championships—had already sensed that East was wavering on his focus on racing. "It was obvious that his heart was not fully into racing, but until he told me his reasons I was in the dark," Carney said. "I told him that I was happy that he discovered something that he was passionate about and that he should pursue it."

Kelly Benefits Pro Cycling Team kept East on the roster for 2011. That left the door open for his return to professional racing. Young men often change their minds, and East still loved bikes. "Although Guy has decided to scale back his racing, this season he'll be representing our team and our sponsors at several events," Carney said.

"If someone is unhappy, I am the last person to try to convince

Author with Guy East at 2010 US Pro Championship in Greenville.
Photo courtesy of Daniel Lee

them to continue. Cycling is a very difficult sport, and if your heart is not in it, you aren't going to be very fast. Being a professional cyclist is like being on a roller coaster," Carney added. "It's a tough job with a lot of highs and lows. So in general it's best to just ensure that an athlete is not making any rash decisions. I always try to encourage them to take plenty of time before making a big decision to avoid having regrets later on."

East now had time to think.

In the weeks after the US Professional Championships in September, East shifted away from the routines of a professional cyclist. He took a break from training. Using an airline voucher he had, East booked a one-way ticket to Puerto Rico in October. He carried some cash, his credit card, and his passport. His backpack carried little more than some clothes, his Bible, and a camera. He would wear his MELLOW JOHNNY'S T-shirt almost every day for the next six weeks as he wandered. He knew some Spanish, but was hardly fluent. East had no plan. But he saw what he was doing as part of his mission in life, or at least a journey to discover that mission.

After starting in Puerto Rico, East would travel to the Dominican Republic. He'd sail on the Caribbean with someone he befriended. He traveled through Haitian immigrant neighborhoods in the Dominican Republic and was gripped by the poverty he saw. He traveled to Panama and in a taxi met a dark-haired beauty named Katrin, who was on a quest to visit two hundred countries by the time she turned thirty. The two travelers were about the same age. They rode horses, saw shooting stars, and swam by a volcano. They'd split up but remain in touch and eventually met up again back in the United States.

East, though, mostly traveled alone while in Central America. He crisscrossed Panama and Costa Rica, taking detours because of mudslides. He'd go on to travel to Nicaragua, Honduras, El Salvador, and Guatemala. East was aware of the dangers of traveling alone. Yet if he sensed he could trust a stranger, he did. Sometimes he was tired and miserable and wished he were home. But most of the time, he enjoyed the adventure. After he mistakenly got off a bus at the wrong destination, a young mother gave him a ride. Shakira songs blasted as the car sped down the road and the mother nursed her fussy infant while driving. East visited an orphanage and missions. In Granada, in Nicaragua, he went with mission workers to a notorious drug neighborhood to pick up men for a Bible study. Dogs ran everywhere. He saw one dog that someone had sliced open with a machete whimpering and wandering aimlessly.

During his travels, East said he met other Americans but didn't connect with them. "There are a lot of backpackers. It wasn't strange to see a backpacker. When I would hang out in the streets with homeless people, the people in my hostel . . . I just ended up not talking to them anymore," East said. "They go and they travel and they see all the tourist sites . . . It's not something I want to do: party all the time. I would go out and just chill in the streets with people that needed to be talked to. I would just pray for homeless people and pray for cities. That the biggest thing I can do, is just praying for them and touching them and spending time with them."

East returned from Central America in time to be with his family for Thanksgiving.

The same adventuresome spirit and cultural flexibility that had allowed East to race bikes and live overseas had helped to safely guide him around Central America. In many ways, East's spontaneous journey did not come as a complete surprise. In August, East had told me how he planned to stop road racing at the end of the season. He talked about how he wanted to ride his bike around the world doing charity work to help the poor. He was still working out the details.

At the time, East's plan was to still race in Europe's fall and winter six-day circuit. Yet that plan, too, had perhaps melted away by the time we met for pizza in late November. He talked about possibly racing more but had no specific plans.

"Do you think you'll have regrets?" I asked.

No, he said. "Being a professional cyclist, for me, was very selfish. Going out and training for six hours a day. And eat this and that . . . I couldn't do that anymore."

What's more, road cycling as a professional had ceased being fun, he told me. Bike racing had become a job. Training in the rain had become miserable.

East, though, enthusiastically talked about the many months he spent as an amateur at the USA Cycling house in Izegem. He spoke of pranks and of loving to talk with Dejonckheere about stocks and business. He told of how some on Team USA would confide in him that they secretly despised racing in Belgium. He never felt that way himself. "We're in Belgium. We're in the heart of the cycling world. We're living our dream," he would tell them. Cycling was East's life. He missed sixty days of class in each of his junior and senior years of high school.

East said one former Olympic cyclist congratulated him on the decision to stop. "He was like, 'Dude, you got out of the tortuous cycle and vortex of cycling.'"

Benjamin King said his close friend East had given a full effort to racing even on his way out. He never slacked in his training. Some questioned East's decision, according to King: "Everyone is kind of like, 'Dude, you don't have a plan. You don't have any support. You don't have any money. This is foolish.'"

Yet King supported his friend. "There are so many guys in the sport right now just dragging it on, just miserable. Props to the guys who have the guts to get out and do something else. I think Guy is following his calling, following what he's made to be."

East—though he may still return—is hardly alone in leaving the professional peloton as a young rider. Injuries and illnesses, burnout, as well as lifestyle and financial considerations are among reasons riders leave the pros.

Former racer Todd Henriksen loved—and still does love—cycling. The Georgia native, born in 1984, first raced mountain bikes with his best friend, BMC pro John Murphy. Then Henriksen switched to road racing, quickly advancing from a beginner Category 5 to a Category 1 racer invited to the US National Development Team's house in Izegem in 2005 and 2006. With his five-foot-six, 130-pound build, he could climb well and also prided himself on his sprint.

Yet Izegem brought frustration and almost constant illness. Not wanting to pass up his opportunity to prove himself in Europe, Henriksen raced with bronchitis—a decision he now believes caused him to develop exercise-induced asthma.

He stuck with cycling. In 2007, he raced for a small US pro team making less than $10,000 a year. Henriksen, who had graduated with a business degree from the University of Georgia, started seeing classmates land business jobs paying $40,000 or $60,000 a year. As with East, Henriksen also came to see his cycling as self-obsessed—his bike and his dietary needs always had to come first.

When in 2008 Henriksen was offered a chance to work for the

Boosterthon Fun Run—a Georgia-based business that organizes fitness, leadership, and fund-raising programs at schools—he took it. Henriksen, who moved to Orlando, also had been working to organize a ministry for professional riders. East was one among a small group of pro riders he met with at the US pro championships in Greenville to discuss his Christian outreach plans.

California Jackson Stewart made it further in cycling than most American pros. He was one of the original members of the BMC Racing Team. He competed in monumental races including Paris–Roubaix and the Tour of Flanders.

Stewart had risen from the US domestic circuit—racing for teams sponsored by Kodak Gallery and the Sierra Nevada Brewing Co.—to sign with BMC after a strong 2006 season. But as BMC transformed itself from a domestic-based squad to a team competing in the Tour de France and other top races, Stewart found himself struggling to step up his own performance each year. He had become a domestique on a team populated with stars including Cadel Evans and George Hincapie.

Jackson Stewart with his son, Zane. Photo courtesy of Jackson Stewart

"I had a great time with the team, and I think I always proved my worth. But I was having a harder and harder time as the team grew to prove my worth," Stewart said. It was a challenge some seasons just making the roster.

By midseason 2010, Stewart knew he was in need of strong performances to land a new contract. At the Tour de Beauce, held in June in Canada, Stewart recorded a second-place and two tenth-place finishes in the six-stage race. It was a solid performance, but when he returned home to San Jose he felt sick. He almost collapsed while out shopping and ended up staying in bed for five days. Soon, though, he was back in Europe, to race in the Tour of Austria. Stewart performed fine, but still didn't feel right. "I was just always fatigued. My head was never clear."

By August, Stewart had returned to the San Francisco Bay area and was seeing physicians to figure out what was wrong. He received no quick diagnosis, but from his own research and from talking with doctors Stewart was thinking it was chronic fatigue. Perhaps Stewart had simply worn his body down by trying to meet the demands of his sport. "You start to push through things that maybe you shouldn't push through, and maybe that's what I did," he said. "Year after year after year, you just keep sacking it up and just keep sucking it in and just keep getting up and going out the door and working hard and doing what you got to do."

All this time, the cycling season was moving on—riders were signing contracts for the next season. Rosters on good teams were filling up without him. Stewart, though, had other options. He had a business management degree from San Jose State, although he said he couldn't think of anything specific he had learned there. His entire adult life had been spent racing bikes; that was what he knew and where he wanted to work. He had been having talks with some of the directors on BMC about eventually becoming a team coach or director. He then talked with Jim Miller, USA Cycling's vice president of athletics, who came back with a specific job offer for 2011—to manage the Women's National Development Program out of USA Cycling's house in Lucca, Italy.

Without a contract and still not feeling well, Stewart saw the opportunity as his golden ticket. In December 2010, USA Cycling announced that J. Stew Inc.—Stewart's business—was the new manager of its Women's National Development Program.

Stewart now had to think of himself as an ex-professional.

"I think I had a good career," he said. "It's funny saying *career* now because I still feel like I'm not done with it, but I am." Thoughts on his career poured out. He was so thankful to have raced for BMC—to have taken part in some of the great races of Europe on a team that paid an actual salary and had a decent budget. He was proud of his skills as a cyclist. He avoided falls and damage to his equipment. He never broke a collarbone, or any bone, from a crash. Once, he tore ligaments in his thumb. In eight years as a pro, his only ambulance ride was for hypothermia during the Tour of California. "I was always proud of that track record."

Stewart also was proud of riding for BMC as his Australian teammate Cadel Evans won the 2010 Flèche Wallonne race in Belgium. He pointed out that he was not at the front of the race for Evans at the end, but he was proud nonetheless.

"BMC was just a journey the whole way," Stewart said. "That's the highlight. In my career, my highlight was that team."

In fact, when I asked East and Stewart to name the best moments of their pro careers, the two riders gave the same answer: They loved the days when the team raced strongly and efficiently together. When they felt like they belonged. "Whenever you give everything you have, you can be really satisfied," East said.

Stewart had taken risks to chase his dream of European cycling. He and his wife, Cherise, and young son, Zane, moved into an apartment in Girona, Spain, to give him a European base. Most of his European racing, though, would be in the tough colder races of Belgium and northern France. Stewart and his family had to move back in with his parents for three months as his cycling career ended before renting an apartment in San Jose. With his new job, he'd make regular trips to Europe but keep his residence in the United States. He was beginning life as an ex-racer.

As Stewart and I finished our conversation, I told him that he had been helpful. I mentioned how, during our earlier conversation in June, he provided me great information on what it was like to race on the roads of Europe, and how he had talked about the awkwardness of being drug tested. I told him I planned on using those things in my book.

"I'm glad to be part of a book," Stewart responded. "That makes me part of history."

What It Takes

At the beginning of this project—before I traveled back to Belgium, before Benjamin King, Daniel Holloway, and Taylor Phinney became US professional champions—I set up a phone interview with USA Cycling Chief Executive Officer Steve Johnson. As head of cycling's governing body in the United States, he was a good starting point for me to discover the pathway to Europe for young American cyclists.

During our roughly thirty-minute phone call, Johnson discussed USA Cycling's developmental programs and how they're designed to build experience by exposing American riders to the rigors of European racing in their teenage years. He talked about the differences between American and European racing. I asked him what qualities he saw in the young US riders who succeeded in achieving the highest level of the sport, the European professional peloton.

What does it take? That was my central question.

"One thing for sure is you have to have the ability. You have to be able to put out a certain amount of power," Johnson told me, adding: "You have to have a great attitude. At the end of the day, you have to like living in Europe."

That, at the most basic level, is the answer. Yet during our phone call Johnson also asked for my mailing address. He wanted to send me a book that had influenced his thinking on what goes in to creating top-notch cyclists. A few days later I received a large envelope containing the five-hundred-plus-page *Developing Talent in Young People*—a book published in 1985 based on the findings of a University of Chicago study called the Development of Talent Research

Project. The study was based on the experiences of 120 people who had reached the pinnacle of their respective areas of study: sculptors, mathematicians, concert pianists, research neurologists, Olympic swimmers, and world-class tennis players. Johnson, though, said the findings applied to the development of bike racers as well. Indeed, the book chronicled patterns also seen in many young elite cyclists: Parents help to introduce and encourage a child in an activity, and after experiencing early success, the child gains motivation to continue improving and developing that talent.

Again and again, *Developing Talent in Young People* noted the importance of support from parents, coaches, and mentors at various stages of a young person's life. This, too, was seen in young cyclists: Benjamin King, Daniel Holloway, Taylor Phinney, Lawson Craddock, and Sinead Miller all talked of support they'd received from their parents. Young pro rider Chris Butler talked about the privilege of training with veteran George Hincapie. These young riders also supported one another. Holloway and Phinney joyously hugged King after he won the US professional road race in Greenville. In Belgium, King pedaled more than eighty miles with an ugly gash just below his knee in large part because he wanted to be part of the team trying to help Phinney win the race. And when Phinney did win on a cold miserable day in Belgium, Holloway raised his own arms back in the pack to celebrate the victory. Olympian Danny Van Haute believed in Kiel Reijnen. My college friend Mario Camacho draws satisfaction from helping young teenagers learn basic pack-riding skills.

The book noted that talented young people—whether they are involved with music, sports or math—possessed similar qualities:

- A strong interest in and emotional commitment to their field.
- A desire to reach a high level of accomplishment.
- A willingness to put in a great amount of time and effort to reach that level.

Brent Bookwalter, who in 2010 completed his first Tour de France, used the term *mental fortitude*. When the pace is hot, when your legs and lungs are searing in self-inflected pain, you have to be able to keep pace with the rider in front of you. Marathons and triathlons are brutal tests of endurance, yet the participants control their own pace. A pack of bicycle racers is more like a Slinky: constantly expanding and contracting as it rolls down the road. Riders may find themselves anaerobic—their legs pumping pedals beyond the capacity of their heart and lungs to keep up with—in the opening miles of a 120-mile road race. If they lose contact with the pack and its protective draft, their race is over. They know the pace will slow, but they don't know exactly when. So they must hold on as long as possible. One rider referred to this as the ability to "nuke it." In professional cycling, the nuclear option is always on the table.

Young American cyclists seeking success in Europe also must be cultural chameleons. Bicycle racing is still profoundly European. Its traditions and almost all of its heroes are European. Americans competing in the sport's biggest events—the Tour de France, Giro d'Italia, Paris–Roubaix, Tour of Flanders—are perpetually playing on the road.

As I planned my trip to Belgium to report for this book, I traded emails with PezCyclingNews.com contributor Edmond Hood, a Scot, asking him the most basic logistical questions on how to watch the Tour of Flanders. How do you get a media credential? What's the easiest way to follow the race? What's the best way to travel between Flemish towns? The logistics were daunting.

"You must see the start . . . The atmosphere is wonderful," Hood responded. He told about the live band, the old streets and square of Bruges lined with fans before 8 AM. It's a scene I tried my best to describe in the prologue of this book.

"It's best not to be too clever and try to see it too many times—the traffic congestion is dire, literally half of the population is out to see the race," Hood warned. When I asked if I could rely on the Belgian rail system for travel, he said: "You can get trains—but ain't none in the carrot fields, dude!

"Try to see it a few times, then 'embed' in a bar or café to see the finale," Hood wrote of watching the Tour of Flanders. "If a Belgian wins . . . it's fantastic."

I heeded Hood's advice as closely as possible. I followed the Tour of Flanders with a Belgian cycling fan and his Dutch friend. I had contacted the man, who with his wife ran a small bed-and-breakfast in Bruges, as I searched for lodging. He had no room, but we ended up trading emails about cycling and he was gracious enough to allow me to accompany him and his friend as they watched the Tour of Flanders.

We saw the start in Bruges's old square. We sat in a bar and ate soup and drank a beer as locals watched the race unfold on TV. At one point during the day, my Belgian host, his Dutch friend, and I were talking about soccer and the World Cup. Yet the Dutch man said he preferred cycling. "Cycling is different," he said. "Before you win, you suffer."

Such a profound understanding of the sport is in contrast with how cycling is viewed by mainstream America.

When they are back home, US pro cyclists often search for basic analogies to explain their sport in terms American media and sports fans will understand. Benjamin King referred to the Union Cycliste Internationale's Pro Tour (in 2011 ProTeams) as the National Football League of pro cycling. King also sought to explain strategy to a newspaper reporter in football terms. The reporter wanted to key in on the finishing time of the race. King instead told him to think of the racecourse as a hundred-mile-long football field on which the cycling teams have to maneuver. The cyclists use their teammates and tactics to score—to win by having one of their own cross the finish line first. The finishing time is of little concern.

I have often compared Belgian's cycling heritage with the rich traditional of basketball in my home state of Indiana. Belgium had Freddy Maertens, Roger De Vlaeminck, and Eddy Merckx. Indiana had John Wooden, Larry Bird, and Oscar Robertson.

It was, perhaps, an appropriate coincidence that my trip to Belgium in the spring of 2010 happened at the same time Butler University in Indianapolis made its Cinderella run to the NCAA Men's Final Four. In the championship game—played in Indianapolis's Lucas Oil Stadium, only 5.7 miles from Butler's home court, Hinkle Fieldhouse—Indiana native Gordon Hayward missed a last-second shot that would have given Butler the upset win over the Duke Blue Devils. Despite the loss, Butler's run whipped Indiana into a hoops frenzy.

In fact, Butler just seemed to embody Indiana basketball. *The Indianapolis Star,* the state's largest newspaper, published a chart showing that of the teams in the 2010 Sweet Sixteen, the two Indiana schools—Purdue and Butler—ranked one and two in having the most in-state players on their respective rosters. Purdue boasted thirteen and Butler, ten.

Imagine the difference between an Indiana kid becoming a basketball player and an American kid becoming a European-based cyclist. A Hoosier youth can reach the NBA playing only for Indiana-based teams—high school, travel teams, and college. It's a difficult road, no doubt. But it's a path that a player's friends, family, teachers, and the general sports fan understand well.

Now consider the road for an American cyclist. Teenagers travel thousands of miles to Belgium. The food is different. The shopping is different. The girls are different. It's cloudy and rainy much of the time. They compete against Europeans who grow up in a society that knows cycling the way Hoosiers know basketball. They must endure what I like to call the Belgian Hammer.

"When you go over there just as a really green American, you just get your face kicked in. You suffer," Daniel Holloway said. "You learn how to survive because every race you do is hard. Once you learn how to suffer and learn how to be fresh to get to the finish, you see the finish of races. Once you see that, then you can start thinking about how to start winning races. There are some guys who go over. They have the talent. They just don't want to deal with a little bit of struggle or a little bit of suffering."

Holloway said he won his first European race on his fourth trip.

Yet for Holloway and the others, the development process is hardly over. They must learn to be steady professionals.

"The biggest thing Daniel has to learn is how to be more consistent. As a field sprinter it is important that he is always in the mix, even when he doesn't feel great. Field sprinting is often a crapshoot," said Jonas Carney, performance director for the Kelly Benefits Pro Cycling, Holloway's team in 2011. "Sometimes on your best day, a break will roll, you will crash, or you'll get boxed in. Sometimes on your worst day, a win will just fall into your hands even though you feel terrible. There is a lot of chance involved in field sprinting, but if you are always there looking for an opportunity, you will win races. If Daniel can do that, he will gain the confidence of his teammates and also learn how to maximize his chances."

As the 2010 season ended, Benjamin King was preparing for the upcoming season with Radio Shack in Europe. He was moving to Europe.

King had almost instantly become known to US cycling fans from his daring solo victory in Greenville. People started asking for his autograph. "It's just one race," King said. In 2011, he would be a champion—but also a new pro trying to learn. Some of King's friends had questioned the wisdom of his decision to leave his studies at Virginia Tech. Yet King had achieved his goal reaching cycling's highest level.

"I am proud of having the guts to take a risk," he said.

Each year, new young Americans take the same risk. Americans have collectively and incrementally learned how to race the European way. Each generation of US riders makes its contribution. The US system evolves. In 2010, USA Cycling's Under-23 Development Program struggled after the departure of founding director Noel Dejonckheere. In early 2011, the national governing body announced

Taylor & Benjamin. Taylor Phinney and Benjamin King,
two young champions. Photo by Darrell Parks, darrellparks.com

that Marcello Albasini, a former Cervélo Test Team coach from
Switzerland, would be leading the under-twenty-three team based in
Izegem.

Soon new young Americans would be headed to Izegem, then elsewhere, for their chance to prove themselves in Europe.

During my visit to Izegem, breakfast was my favorite meal of the
day. I stayed in a small bed-and-breakfast, and on a few mornings a
kindly old Flemish man would set out my meal—coffee, juice, cereal,
meat, cheese, and rolls. He had worked in Izegem's train station. Be-

sides being a grandfather with a warm smile, he was a huge cycling fan who spoke excellent English. One evening, he brought me Belgian Leffe beer to try. One morning, he showed me Flemish sports pages previewing the Tour of Flanders. We talked about Lance Armstrong, Tyler Farrar, Switzerland's Fabian Cancellara, Italy's Filippo Pozzato, Belgium's Tom Boonen, as well as Belgian legend Freddy Maertens. I told him about my plans to write about young Americans racing in Europe. I told him about Taylor Phinney. He was well aware that Izegem was the European base for the US National Development Team. He knew why the Americans had come to Belgium.

At one point we were discussing which riders were poised for results. He lifted his hand and wagged his index finger at me, making his point. "The future is always with the young," he said with his deep and rich Flemish accent.

American riders now were routinely part of such friendly chats and debates among cycling fans worldwide. I drank my coffee and soaked in our conversation.

Riding into the future. Photo by Daniel Lee.

Sources

This book is based almost entirely on my own reporting and observations from dozens of interviews from late 2009 through early 2011, my notes and journals, and observations during trips to Belgium in 1992 and 2010 and to Philadelphia and Greenville, South Carolina, for races in 2010. Sources also include USACycling.org as well as various team and event websites, as well as those noted below.

Prologue
www.letour.fr.
rvv.be/en.

Chapter 1
"The Ballad of Davy Crockett," lyrics by Tom Blackburn, music by George Bruns, Walt Disney Records, 1955.
"What Is VO$_2$ Max?" by Chris Sidwells, *CycleSport* (May 2010): 114–115.

Chapter 2
"Taylor Phinney Triptyque Stage 2A Time Trial," www.youtube.com/user/USACyclingOrg.

Chapter 3
"Hard Men Shed Blood and Sweat to Win on Flanders Cobbles: Sunday's Paris–Roubaix Caps String of Tough, One-Day Classics" by Chris Baldwin, Reuters, April 9, 2010.

Chapter 4
"Preparing Juniors for Racing in Europe," webinar by Benjamin Sharp, USA Cycling junior endurance manager, February 2008.
www.crazyaboutbelgium.co.uk.
www.belgiancycling.be.
"Pez Talk: The Legendary John Howard" by Daniel Lee, www.pezcyclingnews.com, August 24, 2010.

Chapter 5
National Federation of State High School Associations participation data at www.nfhs.org.
www.usacycling.org membership data.
"PEZ Talk: BMC Neo-Pro Chris Butler" by Daniel Lee, www.pezcyclingnews.com, July 2, 2010.

Chapter 6
www.usacycling.org, UCI Continental Teams and Women's Teams information.

Chapter 7
"ESPN.com's Q&A with Floyd Landis" by Bonnie D. Ford, espn.go.com, May 24, 2010.
United States Anti-Doping Agency, www.usada.org.
"Doping Use Among Young Elite Cyclists: A Qualitative Psychosociological Approach" by V. Lentillon-Kaestner and C. Carstairs, *Scandinavian Journal of Medicine & Science in Sports* 20, no. 2 (April 2010): 336–345. E-published March 29, 2009.
"American Christian Vande Velde Eager for Another Giro Jersey" by Andrew

Hood, www.velonews.com, May 3, 2010.

www.slipstreamsports.com.

"Bone Status in Professional Cyclists" by F. Campion, A. M. Nevill, M. K. Karlsson, J. Lounana, M. Shabani, P. Fardellone, and J. Medelli, *International Journal of Sports Medicine* 31, no. 7 (July 2010): 511–515. E-published April 29, 2010.

brentbookwalter.blogspot.com.

Chapter 8

"An American in Belgium" by Daniel Lee, www.pezcyclingnews.com, April 23, 2010.

Cycling Center rider literature.

Chapter 9

Cobblestone Dreams by Brent Bender (Bloomington, IN: AuthorHouse, 2005).

Chapter 10

"Cobblestone Heroism" by Anja Otte, *Flanders Today,* March 31, 2010, page 1.

"Philly Preview: America's Greatest One-Day Race" by Daniel Lee, www.pezcyclingnews.com, June 4, 2010.

"Philadelphia '10: Tassie Rules in Philly" by Daniel Lee, www.pezcyclingnews.com, June 6, 2010.

"Looking Back at 2010 with Brent Bookwalter" by Daniel Lee, www.pezcyclingnews.com, November 16, 2010.

Chapter 11

Sources: "Philadelphia '10: Tassie Rules In Philly" by Daniel Lee, www.pezcyclingnews.com, June 6, 2010.

"Cycling's One-in-a-Million Story: Overworked Wall Streeter Buys a Bike to Stay Fit, Discovers an Elite Talent" by Reed Albergotti, *Wall Street Journal,* August 10, 2009.

Chapter 12

"US Pro Champs TT: Phinney Arrives!" by Daniel Lee, www.pezcyclingnews.com, September 19, 2010.

"US Pro Championships RR: King Triumphs" by Daniel Lee, www.pezcyclingnews.com, September 20, 2010.

"How We Won the Stars-and-Stripes Jersey" by Ben King, September 22, 2009, www.usacycling.org/ndp/NDPstory.php?id=5454.

Chapter 13

"Indy Cyclist Rides in Popular European Sport" by Daniel Lee, *Indianapolis Star,* December 3, 2009, page B2.

"De Fauw Found Dead in Belgium" by Conal Andrews, www.velonation.com, November 6, 2009.

Chapter 14

Developing Talent in Young People by Dr. Benjamin Bloom (New York: Ballantine Books, 1985).

"Home Cookin'," an information graphic by Michael Campbell, *Indianapolis Star,* March 25, 2010.

Back cover: statistics on American climbers of Mount Everest: www.himalayandatabase.com

Acknowledgments

As I started this project, my friend, mentor, and fellow cycling author Peter Nye told me that writing a book requires from an author the same effort that the Tour de France requires of a cyclist. He was right. Nye and many others provided the slipstream for me to complete this project. Thanks most of all to Jennifer, my incredible wife, for helping me in too many ways to count. My parents, Peter and Karin Lee, have always surrounded me with love and support and, for this book, provided me with an airline ticket to Belgium. My in-laws, David and Ellie Gallahue, offered encouragement and ears that have never tired of my cycling stories. To my cycling buddies including Court Maple, Mario Camacho, Paul Didier, Matt Erickson, Brooks Lawrence, and Jim Donatelli—you all helped ignite my passion for cycling, or inspired me to keep that flame burning. Thanks to Tom Davies, Chris Herndon, and Kathleen O'Malley for tirelessly reading chapter drafts, and to my newspaper buddies Matthew Tully and Tom Spalding for insight and encouragement. Sean Weide of the BMC Racing Team, as well as Andrea Smith and Benjamin Sharp of USA Cycling, went beyond the call of duty in helping me gain knowledge, set up the interviews, and make the connections that made this book possible. Thanks to George Hincapie for writing a wonderful foreword, and for entertaining American cycling fans for so many years. Thanks to Darrell Parks for great photos, and to Edmond Hood for photos and travel advice. Thanks also to Richard Pestes of PezCyclingNews.com for publishing some of the features and interviews that are part of this book. I also want to acknowledge the many great colleagues, editors, and experiences I had during my years in newspapers, especially the *San Jose Mercury News* and *The Indianapolis Star*. Lastly, I am especially grateful to the many young cyclists who are featured in this book. Your drive, passion, and perseverance are inspirations.

Giving Back to Bikes

Cycling has enriched my life in many ways for many years. At least 20 percent of my first-year proceeds from this book are being donated to a small number of bicycle-related causes. For more information or to donate yourself, visit:

usacdf.org: USA Cycling Development Foundation. Created to raise money for athlete development programs in cycling for juniors, and men's and women's under-twenty-three programs for young riders to get crucial experience racing overseas.

bikepure.org: Bicycle racing cannot thrive and grow to its potential if it endures seemingly endless doping scandals. Bike Pure is an independent, global organization of fans, riders, and others in cycling who oppose doping and who push for constructive ways to create a nurturing, clean environment for future champions to succeed.

Ride strong and be safe,
Daniel Lee